THE CANCER WHISPERER

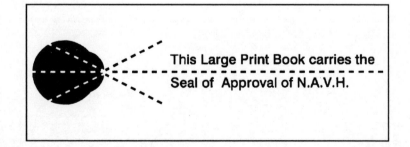

This Large Print Book carries the
Seal of Approval of N.A.V.H.

THE CANCER WHISPERER

FINDING COURAGE, DIRECTION, AND THE UNLIKELY GIFTS OF CANCER

SOPHIE SABBAGE

THORNDIKE PRESS
A part of Gale, Cengage Learning

GALE
CENGAGE Learning·

Farmington Hills, Mich • San Francisco • New York • Waterville, Maine
Meriden, Conn • Mason, Ohio • Chicago

LIBRARY OF CONGRESS CATALOGING-IN-PUBLICATION DATA

Names: Sabbage, Sophie, author.
Title: The cancer whisperer : finding courage, direction, and the unlikely gifts of cancer / by Sophie Sabbage.
Description: Large print edition. | Waterville, Maine : Thorndike Press, 2017. | Series: Thorndike Press® large print biographies and memoirs
Identifiers: LCCN 2016053159 | ISBN 9781410496690 (hardback) | ISBN 1410496694 (hardcover)
Subjects: LCSH: Sabbage, Sophie. | Cancer—Patients—Biography. | Cancer—Psychological aspects. | BISAC: BIOGRAPHY & AUTOBIOGRAPHY / Medical. | SELF-HELP / Personal Growth / Happiness.
Classification: LCC RC265.6 .S23 2017 | DDC 362.19699/40092 [B] —dc23
LC record available at https://lccn.loc.gov/2016053159

Published in 2017 by arrangement with Plume, an imprint of Penguin Publishing Group, a division of Penguin Random House LLC

Printed in the United States of America
1 2 3 4 5 6 7 21 20 19 18 17

DISCLAIMER

This book contains discussions about health issues and medical problems, especially diverse treatments I am trying for late-stage lung cancer. It is not intended as, and is not, a substitute for professional medical advice. Any books I recommend, or links to websites, are intended to share my research but are not intended as recommendations for your healthcare. I am not a physician. If you should have questions about a medical problem, please refer to your medical physician or primary healthcare consultant. In addition, be advised that neither I nor the publisher can be held responsible for medical decisions that you make as a result of reading this book. Please contact your physician before undertaking any of the recommendations I make.

To my soul mate, John Sabbage,
and our life-drenched daughter,
Gabriella —
the best medicine.

And to the late Dr. K. Bradford Brown,
who taught me to find unlikely gifts in
unwanted happenings.

Exceptional patients refuse to be victims. They educate themselves and become specialists in their own care. They question the doctor because they want to understand their treatment and participate in it. They demand dignity, personhood, and control, no matter what the course of the disease.

Bernie S. Siegel, MD

HOLY LAND
SOPHIE SABBAGE

There is a place on the map
where the map runs out.
No signposts or tour guides;
no language to translate
or towns with tidy names.

There is a place on the path
where the path runs out.
No presumptions or premises;
no philosophies to follow
or prophets to obey.

There is a place on the horizon
where the horizon runs out.
No sunsets to end days with;
no tides to tether time
or lines to stay inside.

There is a place on the planet
where the planet runs out.
No countries or covenants;
no laws to live by
or beliefs to become.

There is a place on the map
where the map runs out.

Its roads are made of light.
Its signs point true north.
Revelation rules.

CONTENTS

13

INTRODUCTION

I remember sitting in the radiation waiting room at my local hospital six weeks after I had been diagnosed with stage four incurable metastatic lung cancer. I was about to start radiotherapy to a large tumor on the C_3 vertebra in my neck, which was eating through the bone into my spinal column and causing me considerable pain. I had multiple tumors in several sites — lungs, lymph nodes, bones and brain — but this one was selected for special attention because it was endangering my mobility and threatening my "quality of life."

According to my doctors, saving my life was not an option, so preserving its quality was now their primary aim — which pissed me off. They seemed to be consigning me to my statistical fate without giving me a chance to be one of the few inexplicable ones who beat the odds. They did their best not to use the "d-word" or put a date on it, but the subtext was ever present when they spoke to me: *Whatever happens, Mrs. Sabbage, don't get your hopes up, because you are going to die.* I hadn't even started treatment, but the water of possibility was already closing over my head.

As I waited for the radiation, I was still in shock. I had agreed to do this particular treatment first because turning over at night and standing up from a seated position had become very difficult. I couldn't pick up my four-year-old daughter anymore. I needed some respite from the pain to think, listen, inquire, intuit and somehow, anyhow, *choose* what the hell I was going to do.

I had lost my balance. My hands couldn't locate the banister that helped me find my way downstairs in the darkness. New protocols appeared slowly, like a procession of mourners behind my previous existence: scans, consultations, train rides to London to see specialists, blood tests, insurance forms, lines through pre-diagnosis appointments in my diary (like social events and business meetings), saying the news out loud to people to make it real.

Cancer gate-crashed my shipshape life in an instant. One day I felt normal, the next a single sharp pain in my back revealed itself to be a large tumor pressing on the pleura of my lung. Over the course of three weeks, my diagnosis unfolded in sublimely merciless freeze frames, each one exquisitely brutal in its precision — until finally, on hearing I had more tumors in my brain than they were able to count, the universe popped like a party balloon and lay shriveled in my shaking hand.

As each scan result came in, my life-force faded and thinned like a waning moon. I was coughing blood, becoming breathless after walking upstairs, and losing so much vision in my left eye that I had to stop driving. I was tired and felt cold a lot. Very, very cold. Perhaps it was the doses of radiation from all the scans that sent things spiraling downward so quickly, but fear and shock themselves are powerful forces that ricochet through the body like bullets. It seemed as if the knowledge itself was killing me. As soon as I believed my life was over, it started to retreat into another room, erasing the windows and soft furnishings, folding up my future, putting it neatly in the bottom drawer, dimming the lights, stopping the clock on the wall.

I knew I needed to change my mental landscape if I was going to have any shot at seeing my daughter's fifth birthday or my own forty-ninth. I didn't want to deny what was happening to me, but nor was I willing to comply with the gloomy predictions of my inexorable ending. I felt furious when people started saying their good-byes to me, and I barked at the nurses when they treated me like I was in a hospice for the dying. I wanted to know every detail of my condition and reject everyone else's interpretation of it. I was willing to hand over the outcome to God, but not to my doctors or to statistics. To whatever extent was possible, I wanted to write my own story and I was damned if I was going to inhabit theirs.

My husband, John, came to the hospital with me the day I went through my first radiation treatment. While sitting in the waiting room, I received a deeply tender text from a friend and might not have let my tears roll so freely if John hadn't been sitting beside me. The nurse assigned to my care hurried over to ask if I was okay. Her concern felt suffocating rather than comforting, as if she was trying to stop me rather than support me, as if my tears might harm me in some way, alarm the other patients or, worse, give them permission to cry too. Yet what better time to cry than this? What better time to honor the life that was vanishing in the wake of my diagnosis, to grieve the future that was being wrenched away from me, to wail like a widow for the fading light?

Now was the time not to freeze but to *feel:* to be fully present to my experience; to let every kind text and loving gesture break whatever shell my heart was still encased in; to be awake, aware and alive enough to prize the cherished things that needed remembering and the unrequited hopes that needed grieving. I was conscious of the stoic silence that hung like a thick fog over the radiotherapy waiting room. The numbness. The underground river of unanswered questions. The shy terror. The private prayers. The intensity of a diverse group of patients waiting for some part of our bodies to be burned and some aspect of our mortality to be orphaned.

"Are you okay?" the nurse asked again with more urgency, her anxiety burrowing into my skin.

I touched her hand lightly to comfort her before replying, "I think I might be the only one here who is."

She stepped back, confounded, unsure what to say or how to help if I couldn't be talked out of my tears. Then she slipped away quietly and kept her distance at my subsequent visits to that hospital. I was an anomaly, an unashamedly vulnerable anomaly in a context through which censored sorrow flowed.

Following that day's radiation to my neck, another nurse approached me and handed me a piece of paper. "This is the date of your next appointment, Mrs. Sabbage," she said matter-of-factly, clearly assuming there was nowhere else I needed to be that morning.

I looked at the date, quickly checked my diary and told her I wasn't free that day. And there it was again: visible alarm on the face of a nurse because I had given the wrong answer.

"But it's your radiation appointment," she responded.

"I see that, but I'm not available," I persisted.

Maybe I could have rescheduled whatever else I had planned. Maybe I was being selfish by not fitting in with the system. But something rose up my diseased spine that made me stand firm. I wasn't having it. I wasn't going to be told to show up on command without being respectfully asked if I was available. And if there was a time for being selfish, this was it. Desperately ill as I was, I knew it was vital for me to make my own choices on every step of this journey — to schedule my treatments around my life, not my life around my treatments, to be the author *and* the protagonist of my story. Although I have frequently been advised to prioritize my appointments over everything else (subtext: *or else you'll die),* something more life-affirming and potentially more lifesaving comes stubbornly into play: my fierce, feisty and indomitable sense of self.

I received many more appointment letters telling me where to be and when before my oncologist got the message. It wasn't his fault. It was the system he works in, a system it's all too easy to get swept away by when you're diagnosed with cancer. It moves like fast traffic on a motorway. Before you know it, you're caught in the headlights, with no clear view of what's coming your way. Your diary is filled with appointments, prescriptions are handed out with minimal explanation, and decisions are made on your behalf — all while you're still trying to come to terms with your diagnosis.

When your life is on the line and every decision seems potentially perilous, a lot of cancer patients want the doctors to make their decisions for them. I understand that. And if that's how you want to navigate your journey, then this book may not be for you. But if you have some sense that directing your own treatment, trusting your own wisdom and taking charge of your own care is treatment in its own right — psychological medicine for your cells, medicine that may matter as much as the drugs you are taking and the food you are eating — then I am writing this for you.

This book is for the cancer patient who wants to remain a dignified, empowered human being when your doctors and diagnosis are scaring the shit out of you, you're so shocked you can hardly put your shoes on in the morning, you're caught in the cross fire between orthodox and complementary medicine and, disturbingly, the medical system treats you like a disease, not a person. It is also for the cancer patient who has a hunch that there is something for them to learn, gain or even be transformed by — if they just knew how to relate to this disease differently from the way most of society does. It is for the cancer patient, perhaps any patient, who is looking for another way.

This is part memoir and part self-help book. I'm writing it to help you author your own story with wisdom, realism, creativity and courage. I want to share with you how I am navigating my own way through shock, terror, grief, other people's awkwardness in the face of my prognosis — and how I'm sustaining an ongoing inquiry into the nature, causes, lessons and gifts of this devastating but illuminating disease.

I started writing this book ten months after my initial diagnosis. I am living with cancer, but all my metastases have gone and my primary tumor has reduced in size by 65 percent — progress my medical team unanimously describe as "remarkable." At the same time, as for all stage four cancer patients, I live with the ever-present likelihood that my disease will mutate and march like an army through my body again. My cancer is systemic and incurable, but I am living with it. No, I'm thriving with it. I listen to my doctors, to whom I am grateful beyond measure, and I attend all my appointments. But now I receive phone calls to ask me when I'm available and my doctors *suggest* rather than *tell* me what to do. We have become collaborative partners on my journey instead of staying caught in the top-down doctor-patient dynamic that still prevails in so much of our medical culture.

The fact is, my disease may well still kill me. Indeed, if I line up behind all the statistics, predictions and likelihoods of having stage four lung cancer, I am a certain goner. At the same time, I choose not to

23

line up behind those things. I listen to them, yes, keenly and humbly enough to pare back the crusted layers of denial that shield us from words like "terminal" and "incurable" until we can hear them without breaking like glass. But I choose to get it without giving in to it, to surrender without succumbing, to shout my name over the rooftops of statistics before my identity is submerged in the cold anonymity of numbers. I am under no illusion as to the gravity of my condition, but I am now able to lean ever so gently into tomorrow without fear of falling or drowning or bursting into flames.

I want to live almost more than anything. *Almost.* I dedicate my days, hours and minutes to extending my life, with a fierce and unwavering intention to raise my daughter into adulthood, grow old with my beloved husband, and make the difference I like to think I came into the world to make. But the biggest win is not surviving cancer, as epic as that would be, and as huge as my purpose is to do so. The bigger win is in preserving my personhood, whatever the outcome — that hard-won "I" that neither belongs to my body nor will disintegrate with my body — and knowing that I let it blossom in the face of cancer, even if my flesh withers. The only way I know how to do that is to notice the falcon across the shoreline and the field of possibility on the windblown shore of another country as I steer my ship through this experience, making one brave, faithful and dignified choice at a time.

At the start of this journey my diagnostician, the doctor who reviewed my first CT scan and conducted my bronchoscopy (a procedure that is not for the faint of heart), said an extraordinary thing to me before passing me on to the oncologist:

"Don't become a patient, Mrs. Sabbage. Live your life."

I took what he said deeply to heart. It empowered me to reach for more than outrunning my prognosis — or dying bravely because I believed it. When I was in deep, fresh, hot-off-the-press shock — about to disappear into that starless night where you cannot see or hear or speak for wanting anything but this — that doctor awakened the best part of me. It was the part that knows the future is never written, that everything happens for a purpose greater than my seeing, and that when the shit hits the fan, I can either fall to my fate or rise to my destiny. I think I have been rising ever since.

In this book, I will share some of the

research I've done, the treatments I've chosen, the diet I follow and the resources that have made the biggest differences for me. I hope this information will help you find shortcuts through the mass of information out there about cancer, much of it conflicting. I also recommend specific books and films I consider essential reading and viewing for anyone diagnosed with this disease.

However, I am not a doctor or medical expert of any kind. I am a cancer patient and a facilitator of human transformation. I'm not qualified to help you overcome your condition. I am qualified to help you overcome your *conditioning,* which I believe is also fundamental to the healing process. I can help you *be* well, even when you *feel* ill, and release yourself from emotional factors that may have contributed to your *disease.*

I don't need to add to the library of books already out there about diet, wellness, and treatment protocols. However, I *can* assist you in charting your way through all that data with a clear mind, attuned intuition and robust sense of self. Whether or not you become clear of cancer, you can still become free of cancer. That is, free of the fear it feeds on; free of the deadline it imposes;

free of the power it can wield over your choices; free of the toxic beliefs that contaminate your healing process; free of the perception of inevitability marching you to your fate.

Though I can't offer magic cures or miracles, I hope this book will enable you to find healing you may not otherwise have found. Out of my own experience with cancer, and twenty years of experience of working with people to awaken their minds and free their spirits, I have designed a practical and, hopefully, transformative process that will support you to take radical responsibility for your treatment and unlock the wisdom of your disease. *My main aim is to help cancer patients transform their relationship with cancer such that they are transformed by their experience of having cancer, whatever the outcome, live or die.* So I hope this book will help you experience the vibrancy of vulnerability, the power of purpose, the freedom of authenticity, and the wonder of forging your own path through a dense, dark forest that sometimes seems to offer no respite or escape. Mostly, I hope it will help you listen to your hunch that cancer has something to teach you, if you only knew how to listen to what it is trying to say.

This is what horse whisperers learned to do with horses — understand their language and communicate with them on a whole new level. They tested the limited levels of understanding and took it to a new horizon, working in sympathy with the horse to gain cooperation instead of trying to "break" it through dominance and control. Through the whispering process, the horse "joins up" with the human, willingly accepting his or her leadership and choosing to be guided by them from that point on.

Similarly, we have been trying to break cancer for decades, even centuries, to little avail compared to the progress medicine has made with other diseases. We are in a hostile and adversarial relationship with a condition there is still no reliable cure for. We are aware of contributory factors that lead to cancer, but few irrefutable causes, while the number of people being diagnosed is increasing exponentially. So perhaps it is time to communicate with this disease on a whole new level and take our relationship with it to a new horizon by working in sympathy with it to gain its cooperation. Perhaps it is time to take it off the battlefield and into the classroom. Perhaps it is time to ask not only how we can heal the cancer in our bodies but also what our cancer is telling us about how to heal our lives.

This is my inquiry. I am a fellow cancer patient doing all I can to learn from my disease and change my life because of it. I am gravely ill, yet weirdly well. More grateful to my cancer than afraid of it. Inhabiting a rarefied space between my fierce will to live and my necessary willingness to die. Witnessing the way a bird sings its way toward nightfall and gives itself to the world until its very last note in a flight of perfect authenticity. Wanting to live the exact same way. Inviting you to live the exact same way, however our stories end.

1
THE COMPASS

Being diagnosed with cancer is a multifaceted challenge for your mind, body, heart and spirit. It is by no means only a physical journey, though all too often it's treated as such.

My doctors ask how my body feels, but not how my heart feels. They ask how I'm coping with the side effects from drugs, but not how I'm coping with the fear that stalks so many of my days or the waves of grief that first crashed onto and continue to lap at my shore. Conventional medicine advises me to eat a "balanced diet" of protein, carbs, and vegetables, while assuring me it is fine to eat sugar. My complementary practitioners are convinced that cancer feeds off sugar (among other things) and implore me to cut it completely from my diet.

At first I was overwhelmed. I didn't know which way to turn or what plans to make. I wanted to live, so I needed a survival plan, but I had incurable cancer, so I needed a death plan too. I was the primary earner in my family but was incapable of working, so I put aside the consulting business I had led for twenty years, while I scrambled for dry land in the wake of my diagnostic tsunami. It seemed so symbolic that my eyesight had gone wonky. I could see only a few feet in front of me. Everything got blurry, precarious, vague. My ability to envision the future, which I had always found easy, evaporated quickly, while time fell in on itself and then spread out like sand.

Terrifying as all this was, I was blessed in many ways. I had friends around me who *did* ask what my heart was feeling, and who were willing to dive down to the depths of my fear with me. Also, I had been prepared for this experience, in a sense. I am in the business of awakening the mind and freeing the spirit by enabling people to alleviate unnecessary suffering, unleash their creativity in response to challenging unwanted events, expand in the face of seemingly insurmountable limitations and be transformed by everything that happens — up to and including their last breath. So my journey after the cancer diagnosis began with the skills I had honed over twenty years, a deep faith in whatever hand life deals me, and a determination to let cancer awaken my spirit even if it destroys my body.

I drew on internal and external resources to navigate my way through a dense, dark forest of (often contradictory) elements:

- Shock and denial
- Fear and grief
- The UK medical system
- A multitude of alternative treatments
- Conflicting advice from orthodox and complementary practitioners
- The shock, fear and grief experienced by people who love me
- The multiple possible contributory factors of my disease
- The need for practical, emotional and financial support
- Choosing relationships that truly support me while letting go of the ones that don't
- Making memories with my five-year-old daughter while envisioning giving her away at her wedding
- Putting my affairs in order while doing everything in my power to get well

Today I am writing with normal eyesight and clear vision. I am well enough to write this book and share a program I have created to help others navigate their cancer journeys with power, purpose and auton-omy.

Consider this book a compass to use when you are lost, a means to chart your way forward in any given moment, depending on what is happening for you at the time. Like a compass, it is designed to adjust to your surroundings and circumstances, to help you find your way starting from wher-ever you are right now. Sometimes you will be hemmed in on dark winter nights by trees so tall you can't even see the stars. Other times you may stand in a clearing on a carpet of bluebells, your face stroked by shafts of sunlight on a soft blue spring day. And sometimes you may even stumble upon the source of the stream from whence the whole ocean formed.

I have put the practices of this program in a particular order for the purposes of this book and because they make some chrono-logical sense based on my own experience. For example, I was so ill right after my diagnosis, I needed to *stabilize my body* before I could fully focus on *clearing my mind.*

Although presented in a linear way, this is a circular process. You are likely to move back and forth between different practices. While *stabilizing my body* was my priority at

THE COMPASS

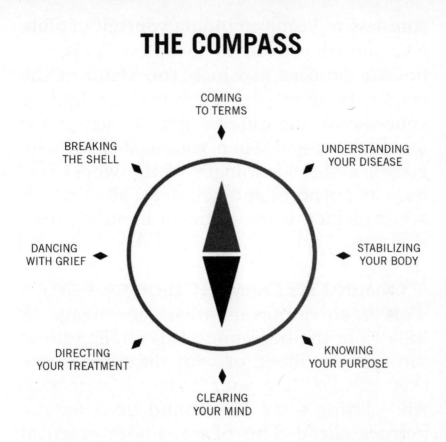

the beginning, it was also a key time for me to *come to terms* with the shock of my diagnosis, which is a critical step in *clearing the mind.* Similarly, I spent many hours a day in those early weeks *understanding my disease* by researching, reading, watching films, googling and talking to experts in the field of cancer, as well as talking with other cancer patients.

Most days, you will know where you need to place your attention, but you can use this compass to keep reminding yourself of what else you may need to focus on. This is a holistic process in which you stand at the center, holding your compass and finding your way to the outer edges of each of the practices, as and when you need their help. Here's a short summary of the whole system, its purposes and key steps, all of which are explained in more detail in subsequent chapters.

COMING TO TERMS (CHAPTER TWO)

This is an important phase to engage in fully from the beginning. It is about getting through the shock of your diagnosis, however early or late your cancer is detected, while laying some firm foundations for the journey ahead. This phase is both practical and psychological. It involves:

a) **Feeling Your Feelings:** expressing and releasing your feelings rather than numbing out and avoiding them, which so often happens when we're faced with shocking news.

b) **Facing the Full Facts:** facing into the full reality of your situation, however hard that is to do, because the more you know about your condition, the more power you have to respond.

c) **Asking for Help:** reaching out to whomever is willing to support you and creating a sustainable support system to facilitate your journey.

d) **Establishing Your Boundaries:** setting necessary limits around your work and relationships so you can preserve your energy for the tough choices and challenging treatments of your cancer journey.

UNDERSTANDING YOUR DISEASE (CHAPTER THREE)

Educating yourself about your particular form of cancer is one of the most important and empowering things you can do after you've received your diagnosis. Either you can leave this to your doctors and do what they say, or you can find out exactly what you're dealing with and what treatments are available (or not). Then you can partner with your doctor, and any other practitioners you find, with more confidence, intelligence and freedom to choose your own path. This phase involves:

a) **Asking Questions about Everything:** engaging in an ongoing, purposeful, brave inquiry into the nature of your condition and what it means for your life.

b) **Doing Your Homework:** researching different treatment protocols at home and abroad so you know your options.

c) **Avoiding Statistics:** staying away from soul-sapping, fear-inducing information that discusses indicators but not inevitabilities.

d) **Tracing the Roots of Your Illness:** uncovering the possible factors that may have contributed to your cancer and being willing to address them piece by piece.

KNOWING YOUR PURPOSE (CHAPTER FOUR)

I often say my faith is the wind in my sails and my purpose is the rudder on my boat. Purpose is a powerful force when consciously chosen and deeply committed to. It will guide all your choices and decisions on this journey, so it's important to get hold of it as early as you can. To survive or to thrive? To hold on or let go? To take charge or be taken care of? To get through this or grow through this? To live or to die? There are no right answers. Just choices. Yours. Boldly and bravely made. This phase involves:

a) **Assessing Your Reality:** reviewing the facts of your illness alongside the circumstances of your life so you can determine the limitations and possibilities with accuracy and wisdom.

b) **Knowing What You Really Want:** engaging honestly, deeply and courageously with what you truly want, given your situation — from how hard you want to fight to how gracefully you want to let go.

c) **Knowing Why You Want It:** discovering your deepest, most heartfelt intentions and envisioning the results you want to create.

d) **Choosing What to Do:** making clear choices and forming a viable, specific and practical plan to underpin your purpose or purposes.

STABILIZING YOUR BODY (CHAPTER FIVE)

This phase will depend on the nature of your diagnosis. If you catch your cancer early, your body may be stable enough to make more progress with the other phases. If you are diagnosed with later-stage cancer, you will need to prioritize this phase accordingly by:

a) **Taking Urgent Action:** identifying immediate things you can do to steady your ship in the waters and catch enough breath to choose your next moves wisely.

b) **Changing Your Diet:** because whatever the arguments for and against "cancer diets," there are too many valid, commonsense reasons to ignore and too many risks to contemplate if you don't change your diet.

c) **Detoxing Your Environment:** creating a context for your journey that is healing, conscious, nurturing, intentional and dedicated to your well-being.

d) **Detoxing Your Body:** minimizing the toxicity in your body so that your cancer has less to feed on.

CLEARING YOUR MIND (CHAPTER SIX)

This phase is all about coming to terms with your humanity, accepting your vulnerability and doing battle with the inevitable fear that grips you when you are diagnosed with cancer. It is also about looking at the fears, feelings and limiting beliefs you may have been carrying for many years but have not paid attention to. In my view, cancer has emotional and psychological roots as well as physical and environmental ones. That is the nature of *dis-ease.* At minimum, it is important to keep releasing the stress that fear generates. If you are willing to go deeper to unblock emotional pathways in your system, then all the better. This involves:

a) **Re-experiencing Your Lifeshocks (significant events):** learning to engage with specific moments in time when you reacted negatively and fearfully.

b) **Killing Your Killer Beliefs:** noticing and tearing down false beliefs (about yourself, cancer, living and dying), as well as assumptions and predictions about the future that generate unnecessary fear and limiting outcomes.

c) **Making Clear Choices:** choosing how to be and what to do in light of what's really true — rather than what you fear, believe, or assume to be true.

d) **Getting Emotional Support:** because there is no better time and no better reason to invest in your mental, emotional and spiritual wellness, in addition to your physical healing.

DIRECTING YOUR TREATMENT (CHAPTER SEVEN)

This is all about taking charge of your treatment plan by feeling informed and clear-headed enough to do so. It is well documented that patients who direct their own treatment fare better than patients who don't, so this is an attitude to adopt as much as a practical plan to put in motion. It involves:

a) **Listening to the Experts:** creating a partnership with your doctors in which you listen closely to their advice, experience and recommendations while asking astute questions and making your own choices.

b) **Using Your Intuitive Compass:** this is your life, and every decision is yours to make on this journey. It's important to start listening to your intuition, that inner instinct that knows what to do when, all around you, people are advising you differently or pressuring you to go in a particular direction.

c) **Creating Your Own Plan:** designing your own plan based on the research you have done and what feels intuitively right to you.

d) **Preserving Your Personhood:** finding ways to remain a person first and a patient second so you stay yourself and maintain your self-esteem in a system that often relates to you as a disease rather than a human being.

DANCING WITH GRIEF (CHAPTER EIGHT)

This is an invitation to completely redefine your relationship with grief and embrace it as a profoundly healing force in your life. Grief is not meant to be held at bay until the end is inevitable or preserved by your loved ones for after you have gone. Nor is it exclusively reserved for those of us labeled "terminal." When you are told you have cancer, grief is as likely to flood your life as much as terror is likely to stalk it. But unlike terror, which tears you apart and shreds your sanity, grief restores your right mind and makes you whole. As well as clarifying its true nature, this chapter gives you three gateways to grief:

a) **Listing Your Losses:** engaging with all the losses, regrets and disappointments you have accumulated in your life but not yet grieved for.

b) **Laying Down Your Regrets:** dispensing with the "shoulds" and "if onlys" that cause untold, often wholly unrecognized pain when we confront our mortality.

c) **Honoring Your Hopes:** allowing yourself to let go of the hopes and dreams that are now genuinely unviable, while resurrecting the ones you still have a real shot at, perhaps especially because you are ill.

BREAKING THE SHELL (CHAPTER NINE)

This is where your work with the previous chapters can take you to a new horizon in your relationship with cancer, by inviting you into a radically different dialogue with your disease, one in which you can find the pearl in the oyster shell, the concealed and unimagined treasures your cancer can offer up when you listen to it very closely and ask what it is inviting you to change in your mind, heart, and being. This is an alchemical inquiry that promises a different kind of medicine, the kind that turns fear into gratitude, sorrow into wonder, and bitterness into hope — the kind that can provide emotional and spiritual healing on a journey of physical healing that has no guarantees.

All of this may seem like *a lot* to take in when you are already reeling from shock — and may also be dealing with physical symptoms that limit your functioning. I remember feeling completely overwhelmed by all the information I was discovering, the advice I was receiving, the decisions I found myself making, and the emotions that crashed through me for many weeks.

So, here's the thing: *You don't need to get this all at once. You only need to get it one step and one breath at a time.* I have designed this process to make your journey easier, not harder. I want it to be as comprehensive as possible to give you the best chance of meeting your needs, but you can prioritize the elements that feel right for you and enlist help if you don't feel well enough to do them.

This system has taken me nearly a year to put together. When I was diagnosed — ten months ago as I write this — it was doubtful I would live much more than a few months, but I am still here. And I am still working my way through and around this program, one shaky step at a time.

I recommend you make your way through this book chapter by chapter, using the compass to navigate your own route through the territory of your diagnosis and how you will respond to it. Above all, listen to life's compass, the unexpected external events that will grab your attention and redirect your choices, sometimes in surprising ways.

For example, I had been focusing more on emotional healing this summer because my body felt so stable, but needed to put emotions on the back burner again when I was taken into the hospital with acutely painful kidney stones. I passed one through my urethra that day, and after a night in the hospital, they sent me home with drugs to manage the pain until the stone still lodged in my kidney made the same excruciating bid for freedom. Two weeks later I was still in pain and felt worn down to the point of desperation. Eventually, a wonderful urologist took pity on me because I had cancer and offered to remove it surgically instead of making me wait for it to pass. I actually wish I had opted for a procedure called lithotripsy, which didn't involve a general anesthetic, but agreed to the surgical option despite my better judgment on this occasion.

Although I'm not sure I chose the best medical intervention, I do know I needed to set everything else aside while I *stabilized my body* again. The emotional work could wait. *This* was the reality I needed to respond to in that moment. After that, I was able to return to attending my heart, *clearing my mind, dancing with grief* and whatever part of the program life will guide me to next.

That is how this process works. It is a compass to guide you when the road ends and the signs disappear. Above all, it is a moment-by-moment partnership between you, your practitioners, and life itself.

2
COMING TO TERMS

The word "cancer" is like a gun loaded with compressed, menacing, terrifying meanings that have stuck in our cultural psyche. When the gun is discharged in your direction, the meanings penetrate deeper than the word itself: *suffering, misery, fatal, hair loss, dignity loss, wretched vomiting, injustice, debilitation, loss of control, incurable, battle, war, life lesson, bad karma, weakness, punishment, pain, disaster, incapacity, protracted painful inevitable gruesome death.*

This is the disease we have been fighting with trillions of dollars and the best of modern science — for decades — and still cannot definitively cure. Its origins continue to mystify. Its causes are too variable to be definite. Its genius capacity to mutate, evolve, and outwit the drugs thrown at it continues to humble and confound the greatest minds in medicine. Curing cancer is the holy grail of modern medicine, and a cure has never been more desperately needed, as nearly 1 in 2.5 people are now being diagnosed with some form of cancer.

"I have cancer . . . I have cancer . . . I have cancer," I kept saying in those first few days after the diagnosis. Part of me wanted to push the news away and bury it in a deep hole in a barren desert on a faraway continent I would never visit. But I knew I needed to get that I really had it. I needed to accept the disease without buckling under its meanings, embrace the reality of my situation without being consumed by its narrative, face into the truth of my experience — not the stories of my culture — and deal with what *was,* not what was *supposed to be.*

All this was as fine a line as I had ever walked. On one hand, I was bombarded with gloomy statistics of extremely low survival rates for people with stage four lung cancer, and patronizingly palliative reassurances about keeping me "comfortable" as I lived out my remaining days. On the other hand, I was plagued by upbeat cancer survival stories that bore no relation to my late-stage, metastatic, incurable condition — as loving, well-meaning friends who couldn't bear to acknowledge that they might lose me tried to pull me into a falsely positive world where cancer never killed, the sun never set, and winter never came.

I didn't *want* to be comfortable. I wanted to be awake, alert and alive to what was happening to me. I wanted to *feel:* to taste the bitterness of regret on my lips; to let fear rattle my bones like the bars of a cage; to catapult my rage at the farthest stars; to break with loving all I would be leaving; to smell gratitude in the pollen of my memories; to stand under grief's exuberant waterfall until it washed me clean of shame.

I didn't want to miss this. Any of it. I didn't want to diminish or dramatize my experience. I didn't want to drown in despair rendered by history books of hopeless cases and inevitable endings, and I didn't want to ice over my abject terror by pretending to be positive about the most devastating thing that had ever happened to me. I wanted to be real about everything, not least the stark fact that I was riddled with tumors and had very little time to indulge in denial. If I had done so, I am certain I would now be dead.

Denial is a deeply disempowering force. It rips you from the truth of things and paralyzes your capacity to respond. It is a temporary shock absorber, a way to keep your horror and sorrow at arm's length while you try to compute the mortality cancer makes you face. And few of us want to face that. We have segregated death. Never in human history has death been more distanced, sanitized, anesthetized, managed, delayed, refuted and closeted away from prying eyes than in this existence-extending culture that exalts youth, vibrancy and flawlessness.

But cancer puts the reality of death in your face. It doesn't matter if your diagnosis is stage one or stage four, like mine. I have met patients who have caught it early on but still stare down the barrel of their own mortality, wondering how hard they will need to fight, how long they will be given, how much suffering they must first endure. It is so easy and tempting to turn away, to tell yourself you will "beat it" no matter what, to put on a brave face for your desperately concerned loved ones, to keep going — business as usual — pretending it will somehow all be okay.

Actually, if you can host this stranger when it arrives on your doorstep, if you can accept the possibility of death early in your journey with cancer, then everything else becomes less painful and daunting to face. It is the outcome most of us want to lower the blinds on until it is literally knocking down our doors. Just talking about it can be seen as giving in.

"You're not going to die," our friends and families reassure us. "Don't even think about that. You must fight this thing."

But dying is not giving in. It is dying. And facing the prospect of dying is not giving in either. It is merely opening to the truth of our nature and the one conclusion we can all ultimately count on as surely as we can count on the sun setting in the evening and the leaves falling when summer moves to the opposite hemisphere. It is the *first* thing to come to terms with when you're diagnosed with cancer, not the last. If you don't, it is always going to be the fear lurking in the shadows, waiting to creep up on you when you go for your next scan or round of chemo or watch your daughter run like the wind at her school Sports Day and wonder how many more races you will get to see her win.

I was lucky. My diagnosis was "terminal," so I needed to come to terms with it quite quickly. There was a short window, after they found the tumor in my lung and before they found the tumors in my bones, where my husband and I could paint pretty pictures in the space between knowing some of the story and waiting for the rest. We started to envision my single tumor being surgically removed, a brief bald period when I would wear a purple wig and write pseudo-enlightened poetry about dancing with cancer, and then the tidy resumption of our cozy lives as if this were just another bridge we had crossed on the road to our ripened and contented old age.

But we knew we were kidding ourselves. We both saw the black clouds forming and heard the low rumblings of a storm blowing in. We knew we were fingering the ragged pages of uncertainty and nestling in its creases where we could cling to each other's safety before the ax of reality fell.

When it did fall, it fell hard. I was a forty-eight-year-old wife and mother. I had met John late in life and Gabriella was conceived against significant odds when I was forty-three years old. The thought of leaving them was almost unbearable. She was four when I was diagnosed and we are very close. I know her little quirks and foibles. I can distinguish her angry cries from her scared cries. I can hear what she is upset about without her having to tell me. I can lean into her shaking sobs and translate them, giving them the words she can't yet form until she lays her head on my assuaging breast and says, "Yes, Mummy. That's why I am upset." No one else can do that for her. Mine are the eyes that see who she is and I don't want to take them away from her. I don't want to leave her to grow up without me. I don't want to miss her growing up.

But I had to face into dying fast because, within weeks of my initial scan, I was indeed dying. There is no feeling like it in the world. It is palpable and undeniable and almost impossible to resist. I remember my life force pulsing away like an unstoppable tide for several weeks and, try as I might, I couldn't stem the flow. There was no avoiding it, really. I needed to put my affairs in order, finalize my will and prepare my family for a life without me. I needed to tell my daughter, who could barely comprehend what I was saying, that I had an illness called cancer and might not get better.

"C for cancer," she said, as if we were just practicing her spelling again.

"Yes, C for cancer," I replied, pulling her to my chest so she couldn't see the river of sorrow falling from my eyes.

This process was an unknown blessing for me. There is so much to come to terms with when you have cancer. I needed to come to terms with stopping work, after having worked all my adult life and been the primary earner for my family. I needed to come to terms with the pain that had moved into my body and taken up seemingly permanent residence. I needed to come to terms with the treatments I chose to undergo in order to prolong my time as much as possible, including radiation and a chemo drug that turned my face into a blistered, acne-covered pizza. I needed to come to terms with more than I could absorb, let alone accept as my new reality. It all seemed way too much.

Hardest of all was coming to terms with my brain tumors. I don't think I can express it any better than I did in the blog I wrote about it at the time:

There are some battles that can only be fought on your knees — usually when you come face-to-face with your own powerlessness, and the only moves you have left are to bow your head in reverence and clasp your hands in prayer. Not the once-a-week-in-church kind, but the kind that eclipses piety and rises from your trembling, tenderized, broken-open humanity like a memory and a thirst.

There are a few times in my life that this has happened — most recently and notably the day I got my initial brain scan results, which was, undoubtedly, my darkest hour. Ever. I recall it like an old home cine film of my childhood, vivid with scratched scenes of indelible memories, each one traumatic and undiluted by the passage of time. I've tried to push it backward into a far-off distant country I don't want to visit again, but it keeps on visiting me.

Yet that was only five months ago.

I was already on a seemingly unstoppable spiral into oblivion when I received the news. By then I knew about the tumors in my right lung, lymph nodes, neck, spine, shoulder, and ribs. I was in pain and fear, each holding hands with the other and exchanging places over and over in a perfect dance. I didn't think I could sink any lower, feel any frailer, or shake any harder. I was at my limit.

I went to meet my oncologist that day to plan the radiotherapy on my neck. He wanted to explain the process, schedule my appointments and make the almost suffocating mask that straps you to the same position on the table for each treatment in order to ensure the laser hits the right spot. John was working that day, so I lined up a playdate for Gabriella and drove to the hospital alone.

Even though I had pushed for a brain scan — because I knew something was wrong — I wasn't expecting the results that day and I never anticipated how devastating they would be. My oncologist "happened to receive the report this morning" and proceeded to tell me what it said.

I was sitting at the side of his desk with my back to his office wall and I had no one to reach out to, as had been the case for all my other scan results. His words blur into non-sentences in my memory: "unfortunately . . . metastases . . . brain lining . . . brain tissue . . . multiple . . . small . . . inoperable . . . radiation . . . whole brain . . . urgent . . . start soon . . ."

My eyes broke like a dam. I was inconsolable. The fear and pain stopped dancing inside me and poured forth. He hardly knew what to say as I tried to stop crying, if only to relieve him of his awkwardness, but couldn't. The tears rolled down my cheeks like monsoon rain on glass windows. Words failed me for several long minutes. What could I say to make the tsunami turn around and drain back into the ocean? How could I un-hear what I had heard?

"How many tumors?" I eventually asked, still chasing the details of my condition as if they held the key to its impossible cure.

"Too many to count," he replied, with a tenderness in his voice that felt like an arm wrapping itself around me so I could weep on its sleeve. "Sorry."

After a while, I stood up to go, but was told

again that I had to leave my car in the hospital parking lot, so I sat down again to figure out how to get home. The oncologist stepped out of his office and a few minutes later his secretary walked in to offer me a lift. I accepted it without hesitation and pulled myself together enough not to scare her while she was driving. It was early evening in November and dark outside. It was dark inside. It was dark everywhere.

Forty minutes later I was sitting on the floor by a log fire in my living room waiting for John to come home. I couldn't phone him or call my parents. I couldn't stand or move or speak.

My brain. My precious, complicated, wise, worrying, poetic, funny, visionary, creative, flawed, fearful, loving, brilliant, exasperating, beautiful brain. Riddled with more tumors than they could count.

They wanted to radiate it, indiscriminately — not target the tumors (too small and too many), but the whole brain. Apparently this leaves you bald for years (if you live that long) and, quite often, permanently. Far worse is how often people say, after full brain radiation, "I'm not the same person anymore."

But then the people who don't have it are often not the same either. The vision in my left eye was already compromised and, while I hadn't wanted to admit it, I was also confus-

57

ing my words and forgetting how to spell. So, either way, it seemed I wouldn't be Sophie for much longer.

I have dedicated my entire professional life to liberating people from the limiting beliefs, harsh judgments and inaccurate perceptions that march us into unnecessary pain and suffering. I have worked harder than most for lucidity of mind, clarity of vision, the ability to draw back the thick curtain of falsehoods that veil life's possibilities and drink from the deep well of Life As It Really Is.

Now my lucidity was under attack, and the possibilities I rely on, even when I can't see them, melted like butterfly wings in angry flames. Without my mind, it was game over. Time to go home.

I used to think people prayed on their knees as a sign of reverence to a higher power, an act of humility. Now I see how sometimes we're brought to our knees by the events of our lives so that we may at last turn our faces to the Light we have never fully bathed in. We pray not to reach out to God, but to let Him in.

By the time John came home I was a calm sea after the storm. Grief-stricken and gutted, but steady on my feet and able to rest in my beloved's arms. Imagine doing this without my babe, I thought. Imagine doing this alone. My situation was excruciating, but I was cradled in love that picked up all my years without him and brought them in from the cold.

In the days that followed I made some tough choices, including refusing to take steroids or have my brain radiated. I also dropped anchor in the fact that I had cancer in my brain and continued, as best I could, with my life.

That was my darkest hour. It was also the day my denial dissolved and my grief began. It wasn't a great flood carrying away the battered landscape of my life on one apocalyptic tide. It was a thousand small waves that washed through my days and caught me unaware in mundane and familiar places. Paying my tax bill. Buying groceries with my husband. Plaiting my daughter's hair. There is so much to let go of when you're told your time is almost up. All of a sudden the third act becomes the last act, this page becomes the final page, the next time becomes the only time, the sometime becomes never.

"Acceptance" is inadequate in describing this process. Acceptance is what you do when you lose a job, fail an exam or end a marriage. It doesn't cut it when you are confronted with your mortality and the loss of everything you hold dear. So I prefer "coming to terms." It allows for an unfolding, an approaching, moving toward something inch by natural inch. It offers a slice of sacred time for shedding the dreams, expectations, hopes and attachments that stand between what you wish for and what is actually so.

This is the passage from no to yes, darkness to light, victim to author, paralysis to creativity, passivity to power. If you can begin by confronting your mortality and facing your fear of dying, then you may cross this threshold more smoothly than if you face that possibility last. It doesn't mean you're giving in. It means you're giving yourself a chance to steer your own journey with cancer instead of fear holding the rudder and blurring your choices along the way. The sooner you can come to terms with your diagnosis, the better your chances at everything: surviving, thriving, living, loving, choosing, healing, learning, changing, grieving, growing, witnessing, wondering, surrendering, creating, laughing, dancing and, yes, if necessary, dying willingly and well.

The rest of this chapter outlines four powerful steps for helping you come to terms with cancer proactively and purposefully in the early days and weeks of your diagnosis. I hope they will help you lay the foundation for all that lies ahead.

FEEL YOUR FEELINGS

Many cancer patients I have spoken to say it took several days, even weeks, for the reality of their diagnosis to sink in. They felt dazed, numb and often worried about the impact on their families more than themselves. Few of us have been taught how to handle fear, so we fight it, suppress it, deny it, control it, put a brave face on it or anesthetize it with a few glasses of wine. Some of us save it for lonely nights when the family is sleeping and we are wide-eyed with terror about all that lies ahead. But it is vital to feel fear, not detach from it. It is important to take the wind out of its sails or it will drive your decisions and blind you to what's really possible. And the only way out of fear is *through.*

This is easy to say, I know. Not so easy to do. I spent several weeks wide-eyed with terror, night after night, not daring to close my eyes in case I never opened them again. I consider myself emotionally intelligent. I teach courses about how to pass through fear and feel feelings in healthy, healing and life-enhancing ways. But this seemed beyond my reach. My cancer was incurable and the chance to raise my darling daughter was being ripped from my adoring hands. How is one supposed to feel in the face of such a realization? Disappointed? Scared? Sad? Those feelings belonged to normality, wellness, being ordinary. They didn't count when I was dying. They shriveled like old apples in the sun, expended and inadequate.

And yet those were precisely the emotions I needed to experience. To process shock, you need to *feel* — be it fear, rage, regret, grief, anxiety, sorrow or despair. If you don't, these emotions will cloud your judgment, drive your decisions and perpetuate your disease. It's simple: *If you don't have your feelings, then your feelings will have you.*

For the most part, this involves letting go of any judgments you have about emotions, so you really get that they are not a sign of weakness but a mark of humanity. It takes strength and courage to engage with them — and a lot of breath!

Try sitting in a quiet place and just breathing into any sensations you feel in your body. Let your breathing expand. Open your throat. Give whatever is there permission to fill your eyes and mark your face. Express these feelings to someone you trust. Talk yourself into them until they overtake your words and leave you trembling, screaming, weeping, wailing, or rocking like a baby in the arms of someone who loves you. Get the feelings *out.*

Above all, get support with this. There are courses you can take, there is counseling you can receive and there are coaches you can hire. If you want to take charge of your treatment, you need to be as emotionally healthy as you can be. I write more about this in Chapter Six: Clearing Your Mind, and I write about how to get emotional support in the supplement at the end of the book. If in doubt, find a therapist and make your appointments with him or her as important as your appointments with your oncologist. There is no better time in your life to do this. I have a therapist and my sessions with him are beacons on my journey where I get to work through the next layer of fear, the next wave of grief, the next blast of anger and the next tunnel of hopelessness or despair. I walk in crying and walk out laughing almost every time.

FACE THE FULL FACTS

The more data you have about your condition, the more power you have to respond with clear choices. When you are in shock, it is easy to settle for what you are told and to assume you're being told everything. Also, when you're scared, you may not want to know more than you already do. You're still reeling. The hits just keep on coming.

You can't take any more, absorb any more, or bear to hear another piece of bad news. It's too much already. I get that I have cancer. The doctors have a plan. That's enough.

Except it's not really enough. It matters to know all the details, however hard they may be to hear. The first oncologist I saw was based in London, but I live in Kent (a county southeast of London), so I asked to be referred to someone nearer home whom I could see on a regular basis. I was happy to see the London oncologist once a month or so, but I didn't want to travel to London more than that when I was feeling very ill. At that point, I knew about the tumors in my lungs, lymph nodes and bones. Specifically, I knew I had them in the lymph nodes in my right lung as well as on my C_3 vertebra, right rib, and left shoulder. When I first met the consultant I was referred to in Kent, he went through all my records with me and mentioned some tumors I was unaware of: some in the lymph nodes in my throat and one on the T6 vertebra of my spine.

I was shocked because that was new information for me, which was partly my fault. I hadn't fully understood the written reports I'd been given. After all, they were full of technical language and I had been in shock at the time. I needed to be told *everything* that was going on and it seemed that my oncologist had left some details out. I called his nursing assistant to find out what had happened and she told me he liked to drip-feed patients the information in digestible sizes so as not to overwhelm them. You may think that sounds quite reasonable, but I was livid. I was literally breathless and coughing blood. I had pain cascading down my spine several times a day and my life force was dwindling at an alarming rate. I did not have time to be drip-fed data about my condition. I needed the full facts — *now.* I needed to know exactly what I was dealing with as fast as possible so I could explore, discern and intuit the very best response I could find.

However scared I was, however grief-stricken about the apparently imminent ending of my days, I trusted reality. I trusted the dark, hard-to-hear, sobering little details of my situation. I trusted that if I could see them for what they really were, I would find a door to walk through instead of an insurmountable wall.

I switched to a new oncologist as a result of that experience. My trust was too shaken and I didn't have time to rebuild it. I stuck

65

with my consultant in Kent, though. He is a gentle man with a dry sense of humor who has worked hard to understand me and respect my need to direct my own treatment as much as I can. Just to be sure I knew where all my tumors were, I stood in his office and asked him to point to each one on my body. He was hesitant at first, concerned it was too confrontational, but I assured him I could handle it. If I have a tumor on my rib, for example, I needed to know which rib so I could protect it when my daughter throws herself into my arms. If I felt pain in my back, I needed to be able to distinguish a spinal tumor from a muscle spasm. If my throat was sore, I needed to know if it was swollen lymph nodes or a simple cold I was catching from my daughter. The data gave me power. It gave me confidence. It gave me freedom to choose.

However hard they are to hear, I urge you to chase down the details of your condition. Don't settle for half-truths and edited information. Don't let your oncologist or doctor protect you from the full facts. Push them for answers until you are satisfied you know it all.

If you are fiercely independent and too proud to ask for help, *get over it.* Now is not the time to show how well you can handle it on your own. Nor is it the time to lie awake at night worrying about how you're going to cope, what you're going to tell the children, how you're going to manage financially or who is going to judge you when your hair falls out. A cancer diagnosis confronts you with your vulnerability and there is no getting around that. It doesn't make you weak; it makes you human. In fact, if you've been mistaking vulnerability for weakness most of your life, you can now thank cancer for slaying that ludicrous lie.

It is time to reach out to those who love you and let them do what they can. They want to, even if they don't know how. When I was first diagnosed, I noticed awkwardness in some of my friends when I told them the news — a look away, a slight stepping back, a wringing of fingers, a prolonged silence, a flush of embarrassment in their cheeks. There was a discomfort in my presence where previously there had been ease, and there emerged a respectful but fearful tentativeness about how to respond.

It is a deeply understandable awkwardness. People want to help, but don't know how. They want to speak, but don't want to say the wrong thing. They want to cry, but don't want to upset you. They want to retreat into their own shock and grief, but don't want to poach your pain.

At first I took it personally and found it hard to understand why more offers of support weren't coming in, but gradually I began to figure it out. They needed me to help them help me. I was the one who knew what I needed, which responses had already made a difference and which ones I had balked at. So I wrote a list for all my friends and e-mailed it to them.

This was it:

Helpful
a) Empathy.
b) Acknowledging I have cancer instead of not mentioning it.
c) Cooking organic high-alkaline vegan meals for my freezer (I can provide specific dietary requirements to anyone who is up for this). I am a crap cook!
d) Childcare (taking Gabriella out, hanging out with her at home so John and I can go out, having her over for playdates if you have little ones).
e) Allowing me to feel whatever I'm feeling,

including hopelessness and fear. Those emotions are appropriate to my situation and don't mean I'm giving up or "letting cancer win." I have spent twenty years teaching people how to pass through fear vs. suppress it, so please trust me if I seem down.

f) Prayers (of the authentic variety).

g) Remembering John and offering to support him too. This situation will put a lot of pressure on him and I don't want him forgotten.

h) Not visiting me if you have any viruses, especially if I am going through chemo. Using antibacterial gel before seeing me, even if you are healthy.

i) E-mailing before you call me so we can arrange a time to talk. Or just e-mail to tell me your news and check in.

j) Telling me about your life. I am still Sophie. I can still listen and my being ill does not mean your lives/concerns are no longer important to me.

k) Forgiving me if I don't respond to your e-mails. I get inundated at times. And tired.

l) Setting up a fund-raising project to help me raise money for the treatments I am unable to access in the UK.

m) Better yet, forming a support team for me and working out a roster of who can do what from the above list in the hard months ahead.

Unhelpful

Everything on this list has all already happened, with the best of intentions, I'm sure, but please try to avoid:

a) Sympathy. I am not a victim and don't see cancer as an enemy to fight. I see it as a huge wake-up call that deserves my full attention and respect.

b) Telling me to be positive and stay positive! (See point e above.) Sometimes being positive is like putting icing on dog shit and calling it a cake.

c) Giving me advice.

d) Telling me cancer survival stories, unless they are stories about multi-sited, systemic, stage four, metastasized cancer that closely resembles my own.

e) Telling me about your non-life-threatening ailments and how awful they are.

f) Analyzing why I have cancer and what my karma is (very high on the annoying scale).

g) Treating me like my days are numbered and I'm at death's door (unless I really am).

h) Expecting me to operate as normal in terms of social activities and general engagement with everyday things.

i) Pretending this isn't happening and carrying on as if it isn't.

j) Taking offense if you offer me something healing and I say no. I need to choose what feels right for me, as well as be selective with my energy and time.

k) Drinking champagne in my presence, making fresh coffee in my kitchen and eating chocolate cake within a hundred-mile radius of me.

l) Thoughtlessly telling me about the people you know who have died of cancer (which is the last thing I want to hear).

It made a massive difference. The support I received from that point on surpassed all my expectations and played a huge part in getting me through those first traumatic weeks. The awkwardness dissolved like salt in water and they thanked me for making it so much easier for them to help, which is what they were longing to do. A support team came together rapidly to coordinate everything I had asked for, as new friendships were forged between people from different areas of my life. One couple filled my freezer with a two-month supply of organic food and bought me all the kitchen gadgets I would need to sustain my new diet. One friend just moved in for six weeks and refused to leave until my house was detoxed, every supplement was labeled, and the terror had receded from my eyes.

In the presence of such generous responses, all doubts that you are loved and lovable, which most of us carry, dissolve into dust and heal old wounds you didn't know were still bleeding. Suddenly, remorse retreats into the shadows, and the affections of your life prevail.

So relieve yourself of your awkwardness and then relieve your friends of theirs. Don't wait for them to figure out what you need. *Tell them.* Write your own list and send it to everyone who loves you. Help them to help you when you need it most.

Fund-raising

I also asked for specific help with fund-raising, because the alternative treatments I believed I needed were beyond my financial reach. Some of them are very expensive, so this is another area you may need to reach out for assistance with. These are my recommendations about how to approach it:

1. Get clear about the amount you need to raise and what it will cover.
2. Write an honest description of what you need and why — or ask a loved one to do this for you.
3. Invite a few close friends to lead the fund-raising initiative for you and make requests on your behalf.
4. Give them a list of people to approach who you believe would be willing to

contribute to your medical fund. They can then write to those people and follow up with phone calls to answer questions and address concerns.

5. Set up a clear payment system — something like PayPal — and a medical account that is separate from your personal and business accounts so you can track the use of your gift money with integrity.

6. Investigate different fund-raising websites like Just Giving, Go Fund Me, and Indiegogo to see which one will serve your needs best. Then create the relevant page on your chosen site. This is very simple to do. You can also look at Crowdfunding.

7. Promote your online page by using social media, like Facebook, to invite your friends to contribute. Your fund-raising team can also promote it on their pages and you can also ask your friends to share the link with other people.

8. If you have a blog or website, put a link to your fund-raising page on your site.

9. Create a way to let people track your progress. This may be by sharing updates on Facebook, your blog, your fund-raising page, or all three. Remember, you can also ask a family member to do this for you if you feel too unwell.

10. Create a way to thank people for their

contributions, such as personal e-mails or personal responses sent from your fund-raising page.

ESTABLISH YOUR BOUNDARIES

Just as you need to get over your independent pride by asking for help, so you need to get over any tendency you have to please, appease or put others' needs before your own. You need to know who your true friends are at this time, who is there to serve, support and uphold you as you embark on this journey. You need to dispense with hangers-on, people who compete with you for attention and people who want to *be seen* to be supporting you because it looks good for them to do so. Yes, there really are people like that.

You don't need to be rude or unkind. You need to be firm. It may be as simple as asking people to e-mail instead of phone you. It may be that you need to say no when friends invite you out to "cheer you up," because you don't want to watch them all having fun at the bar while you're worrying about your next scan results. You might need to ask friends not to bring their infection-prone kids to your house when you're going through chemotherapy.

I have a dear friend named Catherine Rolt

who has lived with a debilitating disease called Ehlers-Danlos syndrome, a connective tissue disorder that weakens and destroys collagen, all her life. She has had nearly thirty operations on her spine, is held together with metal, and has outlived her sell-by date by about fifteen years. She also radiates wellness through her strength of spirit and a rare shining faith honed by decades of physical suffering. So when John needed to stay home to look after our daughter, Catherine was the person I wanted at my appointments, consultations and scan results. I knew she could guide me emotionally and spiritually with love and objectivity, which was what I most needed.

At first this was hard for my parents to accept. Understandably, they wanted to be there with me and felt hurt that I favored a friend they hadn't even heard of. They were family, after all. But I held the line. I needed to do what was right for me, even if it upset them. So my devoted dad, who got it after some explanation, would sit patiently in the waiting room while Catherine and I were with the oncologist, eager to be updated afterward and determined to give me a hug, whatever the news.

The hardest boundary for me to hold in the months after my diagnosis was with a very old and close friend with whom I had fallen out about nine months before I discovered my cancer. The details of why don't matter except to say that we both hurt each other quite deeply and our differences had never been reconciled. These differences were both personal and professional, our having worked together for many years. On hearing I had cancer, she wrote me a loving letter asking to reconnect with me and "find solace in one another" as we had for so many years prior. At first it seemed wise to do so, not least because I was dying a little more each day at the time, and I wanted to leave with peace between us.

Yet I felt deeply vulnerable and was still bruised by what had happened. I didn't want to set myself up for more hurt or simply step back into friendship as if things were the same as they were before. I didn't want my cancer to camouflage the bruises or become a get-out-of-jail-free clause for the things we both needed to apologize for. Above all, I had no time for pretense. I wanted truth more than peace, authenticity more than solace — and didn't see how to have the latter without the former in either instance. My condition didn't delete the past or diminish the depth of our differences. It simply called us out to address them once and for all.

As such, I eventually asked her to meet me to review what had happened between us and clear it up through a conflict resolution conversation, something we both teach others to do. I even suggested we meet with a mediator because it was bound to be a difficult dialogue. When I asked, I think I said some more hurtful things to her, which I also regret. I was ragged in my body at that time and that raggedness leaked into my words through some pissy remarks and premature feedback, which were better left omitted until we met in person. My intent was never to drive a bigger wedge between us but to own what we had done to each other, then lay it to rest or let the relationship go.

In the end, she chose not to have that conversation with me, declaring there was "too much water under the bridge" for that to happen and requesting that there be no further communication between us. That was a truly sad day for me. I wondered what would have happened if Mandela had said there was too much water under the bridge to reconcile with de Klerk. There is never too much water, in my view. At the same time, I recognize how I provoked her to back off more than I encouraged her to come forward. I was sorry for this too.

I still feel sad as I write about this. I have not forgotten who she was to me or how much I loved her. I miss her deeply some days. She was my go-to person for nearly twenty years, the one who wiped snot from my nose and tears from my eyes on numerous occasions. But I don't regret refusing to gloss over our conflict or holding out for a friendship without undercurrents of animosity when I most needed to feel safe.

That decision released our relationship from the holding pattern it had been in for more than a year and, in turn, released more of my energy for emotional and physical healing. So I gave it to the river of grief that has merged with my bloodstream and flows like oxygen through my beckoning life.

I also feel unexpectedly grateful for the way she left my life so permanently. At a human level it was deeply hurtful, but at a soul level it was remarkably generous because it freed me to move into a completely new sphere of friendship, vocation, and service that I may not otherwise have moved into. I will always honor her for this.

You will know where your boundaries are. You will find them at the edges of your vulnerability — softer than walls that defend and hide you, but firm nonetheless. They mark your physical and emotional limitations, the outer rim of your humanity, where you recognize what you're capable of and what you're not. They are the containers within which you can let your heart shatter into a thousand pieces, certain that you are still whole and loved and safe.

3
UNDERSTANDING YOUR DISEASE

Before my diagnosis I knew very little about cancer. I knew it killed more people than any other disease. I knew it was treated with surgery, chemotherapy and radiation. And I knew it had four stages, the last of which is defined as systemic and irreversible. That was pretty much it. I had known people who'd died from it, and others who'd survived, including both grandmothers, one of whom had a mastectomy at fifty and lived into her seventies. My mother also came through breast cancer in her sixties, having caught it early. Genetically speaking, breast cancer was the type of cancer I was most likely to get. I'd even had a mammogram for a lump I found two years before I discovered I had lung cancer.

It is very easy to take the information you are given at face value and assume your oncologist knows everything there is to know. As you stare into the blinding headlights of a cancer diagnosis, you're likely to have one burning question, the answer to which will dim the lights and help you see the road ahead: *What the hell do I do now?*

At first, I was offered palliative care, which included radiating the tumor on my C_3 vertebra to relieve the pain and interrupt the looming threat to my spinal column. In addition, they would try chemo to buy me some time and manage my pain, but other than testing me for unlikely genetic mutations, there was little more they could do. In my despair, which trampled across my cratering chest like an army marching through the desert, I asked only one other question that day.

"How long do I have?"

There seemed to be nothing else to ask. No options to explore. No alternatives to consider. Just how to prepare to die. I've always questioned everything and lived my life in inquiry, continually opening myself to what I don't know. But my curiosity wilted like weeping petals falling onto a parched flower bed, conceding to the natural order of things as I summoned just enough courage to face my demise.

It wasn't entirely defeatist. I wanted to be proactive, to paint my last days in glorious technicolor, to heal wounds I had left open, repair relationships I had broken, bring some semblance of peace to all the jagged corners of my soul.

I wanted to make videos for Gabriella that she could watch while growing up without me, a whole series that would span the seminal moments of her life when she might wonder what her mum would say about this or advise her about that. Leaving primary school. Being bullied or rejected. Menstruating. Developing breasts. Her first crush. Doing something unpopular to be true to herself. Falling in love. Losing her virginity. Having her heart broken and fearing love will always break it. Graduating university. Figuring out she is gay or feeling certain she isn't. Becoming a fireman (which is what she aspires to be now). Winning an Olympic medal (which is what her proud mum imagines her achieving whenever I watch her run). Failing at something she worked so hard for, the disappointment sticking to her gut like tar. Discovering her heart can't break from loving but from fear of loving. Getting married. Feeling her firstborn's skin against her skin and wondering if I had felt this much awe when I first felt her skin against mine. Losing her dad, who had raised her so bravely without me, and feeling the same grief that ruptured her childhood batter her heart like hail. Seeing both our faces in the eyes of her children and in the light of a thousand stars. Realizing that grief is not a temporary emotion that eventually recedes into forgetfulness, but a way of continuing to love whatever has slipped through the curtains, of bearing faithful witness to the stories that marked her soul.

I was making that list in my head on the two-mile journey from the oncology unit to my friend's apartment nearby, realizing that I wasn't afraid of the actual act of dying but of disappearing, of fading like a mist from the memories of my beloveds, leaving an earth washed clean of my presence and its amassed graces because I'd failed to take root in the world.

Mercifully, my oncologist never answered my question. He said he would hazard an educated guess if I pressed him to do so, but I didn't. I thought better of it and felt grateful he hadn't burdened me with a use-by date. I wonder if I would be dead by now if he had, like the opposite of the placebo effect, whereby, if you believe the pill works, it does. Similarly, perhaps if you believe your game is up, it is.

Instead, he gave me a window of time within which to shift my own perceptions and widen my thinly narrowed perspective. I spent that afternoon in the company of two friends who let my grief roar like a rushing river past all the places I had been shipwrecked and scattered and made whole. I didn't want to die. I didn't want to leave yet. I wasn't ready to relinquish the confounding wonder of my love-stained flesh-and-blood existence or give in to certainty after teasing the threads of revelation from life's cloth. No. My inquiry was not done. The future was not written.

So it was back to school again.

From that point on, I spent hours each day researching cancer on the Internet, reading books, watching films, talking to experts, listening to other patients, trying to filter sanity from quackery, distinguishing the data that ensnared my desperate mind from the possibilities that made sense to my soul. During that time, information came to me from unexpected and mysterious sources. A whole series of synchronistic events directed me to treatments I would never have looked for and delivered answers to questions I would never have thought to ask. It was extraordinary.

For example, I googled "colonic irrigation" and intuitively chose someone from the long list of options I found. When I called her, she had just finished a session with a client who had recently returned from a clinic in Mexico, fully cured, after previously having been given only three months to live in the UK. She told me this woman had found out about the clinic in Mexico from a film called *Cancer Conquest,* produced by Burton Goldberg. I ordered it immediately and I recommend you do the same thing as soon as possible (www.burtongoldberg.com). It was a game changer. Goldberg made a documentary about pioneering oncologists and clinics offering treatments outside the orthodox "cut it, burn it, poison it" paradigm. I would never have known to look for it, but it seemed to have looked for me.

As a result of watching that film, I sought out Dr. Dana Flavin, who was featured in it and whom I felt deeply drawn to. She runs the Foundation for Collaborative Medicine and Research, a nonprofit organization dedicated to "reading and researching all published information on cancer and autoimmune diseases." A one-off donation to her foundation secured me a two-hour Skype consultation and ongoing support via e-mail. She has worked with cancer patients for thirty-seven years, integrating synthetic and natural treatments in a very refreshing way and shortcutting the arduous challenge of having to do one's own research when very ill. At one point during the consultation, my husband came into my office to say hello and thank her for her support.

"Let's get her well," she responded, "and then . . ."

I didn't hear the rest of the sentence. She was the first doctor to suggest the remotest possibility that I might get well and, when she did, something crossed over inside me. She wasn't blowing any trumpets or making any promises, but from that moment I could see tomorrow again.

Similar things kept happening. It was as if life itself met my purpose to look for more answers by rolling out the red carpet and walking me straight through the madding crowd. It reminded me, poignantly and poetically, of a quote from Goethe I used to share on a transformational workshop I facilitated many times:

The moment one definitely commits oneself, then Providence moves too. All sorts of things occur to help one that would never otherwise have occurred. A whole stream of events issues from the decision, which no man could have dreamed would come his way. Whatever you can do, or dream you can do, begin it.

Boldness has genius, power and magic in it.

I committed to understanding my disease, to leaving no stone unturned in my search for a life fully lived, and providence moved too. I can't possibly know how long I have left to live and my search has not yet led me to a cure, but I have embarked on a great expedition, a road less traveled, an unexpected pilgrimage into the untamed wonder of pure uncertainty, of truly, deeply not knowing what tomorrow brings. My cancer diagnosis was a beginning, not an end, the start of a quest into who I am and what I'm really made of, a living of every moment *now*.

The more I learn about cancer, the less I see it as something to fight and beat. I hear those words used so often in this context. I see posters in London tube stations about "the war on cancer" and frequently hear other patients speak of their "battle" against this disease.

Indeed, this is how it is reported in the press, almost invariably. When someone survives, they "won the fight," and when someone dies, they "lost their brave battle." This is an extremely limiting way of relating to cancer, which does a great injustice to all the mental, emotional, and spiritual victories cancer patients achieve from the moment of diagnosis — whatever the ultimate outcome. It sets up late-stage (i.e., incurable) patients as failures before they have even begun their often remarkably courageous and dignified journeys. And it is one of the primary reasons I am writing this book.

This is how most of society, especially the media, engages with cancer — on the battlefield and in the trenches, doing all we can to annihilate an enemy in a war that seems to have no end. For me, this is cognitive dissonance. At one level, I get it — I'm in it — but at another, it slights my soul. If cancer is the enemy, we are either its victim or its attacker. There is a wall between us, but no door. No dialogue. No listening to what cancer has to teach us. No chance of reconciliation or peace.

I have been at war with my body most of my life, at least since premature womanhood abducted it when I was ten years old, when I didn't understand why breasts had sprouted on my child's chest and blood was suddenly streaming down my legs. Maybe sooner. I used to think my eating disorders began in my teens, yet by the age of eight I was stealing money from my mother's purse to buy chocolate on the way home from school, so maybe my self-loathing had deeper roots than adolescent awkwardness.

No matter. It all seemed to catch up with me when I was bent double by my diagnosis and a thousand "if onlys" trampled like bandits through my past. I was as infected with regret as I was with tumors. I was finally done doing violence to my body. Cancer called a halt to it once and for all. It was at last time to make peace, not war.

From what I understand, cancer cells are normal cells that have been rejected by their host. They are outcasts, deprived of nourishment and support. So they try to survive in a hostile environment, feeding on anything they can find to live on — toxins, pesticides, narcotics, anger, fear, resentment, self-recrimination, guilt, depression and remorse. Discovering this led me to ask some pivotal questions in the way I related to this disease:

What if cancer is the body's last attempt to save its own life?

What if its purpose is not to extinguish us but to close whatever wounds we left open?

What if cancer longs to be loved, like all the cells in our bodies need to be cared for?

What if we stopped hating cancer and started leaning into what it has to teach us about who we are, how we've lived, and what we might yet become?

We can't heal on a battleground. We need

to stop fighting and shake the enemy's hand.

Understanding your disease is not just a matter of understanding its biology and its treatments. It's a matter of understanding what it has to show you about yourself. In my experience, cancer is a great awakener, a siren continually calling me home. I cannot afford to be at war with my own body anymore. I am finally learning to nourish, uphold, prioritize, dignify and appreciate it. I want to get rid of my cancer, but I don't want to "battle" it. This doesn't mean being passive, by any means. It means adopting a different attitude to warfare and becoming a peacemaker in the battle between my own cells.

My quest to understand my disease has led me to conclude that cancer is a symptom of other causes, the manifestation of deeper, underlying *dis-eases* I have been living with for decades. It is a call to consciousness, an opportunity to change the way I treat myself and interact with my environment. My doctors can treat the symptoms — i.e., my tumors — by using radiation and a specific tumor-inhibiting drug I qualified for when they detected a particular mutation called EGFR (epidermal growth factor receptor), which is more commonly found in East Asian populations than in the U.S. or

Europe. And there by the grace of God go I. But these tumor inhibitors have a limited shelf life, especially for a stage four patient, and I don't want to rely on some new miracle drug maybe-just-maybe coming on the market in time to save me when this one stops working. No. My job is to address the underlying causes that put me in this position in the first place, to create the conditions in my body, mind and spirit that make it difficult — perhaps even impossible — for my cancer to reassert itself and claim dominion again. This is the most proactive, loving and peaceful response I can find.

HOW TO INVESTIGATE YOUR DISEASE
To assist you in investigating your cancer, both in terms of how it presents itself and what its underlying causes may be, here are four simple and powerful ways you can gain the knowledge you need to take action:

Ask Questions about Everything
This is key. The more you understand about what you are dealing with, the better you will deal with it. No question is stupid, unnecessary or too late to ask. *This is your life.*

At my early appointments, I was often too stunned to think of what to ask, then questions would stream through my head afterward. I started writing them down prior to my next consultation so I wouldn't forget them. I would also go through them with whoever was coming with me — usually my husband or my amazing friend Catherine — so they knew in advance what I wanted to ask. Even when I had my questions on paper, fear sometimes made me forgetful during the consultations or I would doubt the validity of my questions in some way.

Here are some of the questions I asked my oncologist during the three weeks it took for my diagnosis to unfold:

- Do I qualify for any clinical trials?
- Why can't you operate or do a lung section?
- What about a lung transplant?
- What is the meaning of my genetic mutation?
- How effective has this treatment been previously?
- Why did my neck pain come on so suddenly?
- Why has my eyesight gone blurry on the left side?
- Should I have a flu shot this winter if I am going to have chemo?
- Why do you want me to take steroids?
- How many tumors do I have in my brain?
- How big is each tumor — exactly?

- Can you MRI my chest instead of doing another CT scan? (An MRI is magnetic resonance imaging technique, which uses strong radio waves and magnetic fields to produce detailed images of the inside of the body. It's very noisy, but it's not radiation. A CT scan, also known as a CAT scan, uses combinations of many X-ray images and does involve radiation.)
- Why are the treatment options so limited?
- Why aren't you offering me immunotherapy?
- Do you know about *x, y,* and *z* treatments in Germany and Mexico?

Later, as my body began to stabilize, I paid attention to everything in more and more detail. I asked for copies of all my scan reports and analyzed them carefully. I still do. My husband and I would ask about (or google) any word we didn't understand.

- What is "hilar adenopathy"?
- How can the cavitating lesion shrink and the soft tissue increase?
- What exactly has "improved" about my T6 lesion? Is the tumor still there or is it just scar tissue?
- What are "florid inflammatory changes in the left maxillary antrum"? (Slight swelling in my nostrils, as it turned out!)

I leave no stone unturned. At one point,

my oncologist left a message about my latest scan, saying, "Your brain scan is fine, Mrs. Sabbage. Carry on as normal."

He honestly thought that was all I needed to know! I couldn't believe it. I didn't want to know my scan was "fine" (though that was heartening information, to be sure). I wanted to know what "fine" meant. Had the lesions shrunk or disappeared? Did I still have metastases or traces of metastases? What *exactly* was going on in this extremely valuable part of my anatomy? Don't give me "fine"!

After I interrogated him, he told me that many patients don't want to know the level of detail I ask for. They are content to know the result is "good" or "bad" and to be told what to do next, which I found quite hard to comprehend. He's got me now, though. He puts the scans on screen when I arrive in his consulting room and goes through the report word by word until I am satisfied I understand it. Some answers to my questions can be hard to hear, but I need to know the truth, the facts, the nitty-gritty details of my reality if I am going to find my most effective response.

When I explore complementary treatments, I take the same approach, asking every question I can think of, as if I have embarked on a fast-track PhD in stage four adenocarcinoma lung cancer. I will continue to do so and I won't stop. As long as I have cancer in my body, I will have questions on my lips.

But asking questions is not solely an academic exercise. It is an inquiry of the soul. You not only need to ask questions of your health practitioners; you also need to ask questions of yourself. That is the difference between researching your symptoms and researching their causes, between fixing your problem and restoring balance to your life. Here are some of the questions I recommend you ask yourself:

• What does cancer mean to me and how do I feel about having it?
• How is my perception of cancer shaping my response to cancer?
• What is my body trying to tell me about how I have treated it?
• What part have I played in my body's developing cancer?
• What contributory factors set my cancer in motion?
• How can I restore wholeness to my mind, body and spirit?
• What inner conflicts and unresolved issues have I failed to heal?

This is not about blaming yourself! Please

don't add that toxicity to your precious psyche at this difficult time. This is about being conscious, proactive and response-able. These are the kinds of questions that will enable you to truly understand your disease and, through understanding it, harness some healing and power. You may or may not "beat" cancer. That outcome is a very long shot for me. But I am not a *victim* of cancer. I am not being *beaten* by cancer. I am letting it awaken, heal and transform my mind and spirit. I am more, not less, of myself because of it. It may yet shorten my lifespan, but it is extending my aliveness by many, many miles.

Do Your Homework
This is simply a variation on the theme of inquiry into your condition. As well as asking specific questions, it is important to do as much research as you are able — or enlist support from your loved ones to help you do this.

After my diagnosis, I spent hours a day on my computer. I could barely walk up the stairs and was losing my ability to spell, but I sat by the real log fire at home in those cold winter months — reading, googling, viewing, investigating, and educating myself as fast as possible. I was extremely motivated by the fact that I was sliding downhill faster than a teenager on a skateboard and it was clear I did not have long for this world if I didn't take some drastic action.

Some days, doing my homework was like wading through molasses. I was cloaked in sorrow so heavy I could hardly move my fingers across the keyboard or turn the pages of a book. Some days, I even asked my husband to read something for me and boil it down to its essence so we could continue collating data in my cancer research journal. Other days, doing the research felt like skating on a frozen lake on a crisp, blue winter's day. I would push off in one direction and glide into unexpected information that was exactly what I needed to discover. It was as if a greater force was guiding me to the practitioners and products that could walk me straight out of hell.

Gathering information was a long haul, with a lot of dead ends and dross information to sort through. At times, I felt very frustrated and angry, believing I was wasting precious time reading rubbish blogs, bizarre theories, and false promises of miracle cures. I wished someone had done the sorting for me and distilled it into a single book or document that simplified the whole process. That was hard to find, though, because there were so many conflicting positions, especially between orthodox and complementary treatments, and I was keen to discover all I could about both.

I can't provide that book for you, not least because there are so many books out there about the disease and its treatments. Mine would likely get lost in the forest. This is why I have chosen instead to write about how you can navigate *your* cancer journey, in the hope that it will offer an integrated map of the territory — mental, physical and emotional — and ease your passage in some ways. However, I can recommend some sources of information that made the most difference to me in various areas. You will find them in the supplement at the end of this book, called Support Systems.

Avoid Statistics

There are exceptions to every rule, like this one when you are researching your disease: *Don't look up, look at, or listen to statistics. Just don't.*

So, here's why. *You* are not a statistic, but the moment you buy into the statistics, you are more likely to become one. They are frightening — in some cases (like mine) horrifying — and you do not need fear and horror in your precious cells and bones!

Those little numbers infect your mind as surely as cancer has infected your body. I am the greatest exponent you will ever meet when it comes to embracing reality, but statistics, while representing some past realities, *are not reality.* Your unique outcome cannot be determined or predicted by what has gone before.

Statistics are indicators, not inevitabilities. When I think about the statistics for my strain of cancer (having made the mistake of looking at them before I realized it wasn't helping me), I immediately needed to rip them from my panicking brain and remember that someone has survived every cancer there is, however advanced or "incurable" — including glioblastoma multiforme, otherwise known as "the terminator." Due to the statistics in my case, my oncologist likes to remind me that no one has ever gone into remission on the drug I am taking. In fact, he also says there is no such thing as remission once your cancer has reached stage four. When I shared this with Dr. Contreras, who runs the Oasis of Hope Hospital in Mexico, right after he had reviewed my recent impressive scan results, his eyes twinkled with pure possibility.

"Sophie," he replied, "just remember, very few patients do all the other things you are doing and this drug hasn't been tested on *you*."

From that point on, I stopped engaging with statistics. Dr. Contreras helped me gain the perspective that my journey is *my* journey. All I can do is walk it with passion, purpose, patience, and gratitude for every day I am given. I live my own narrative, not in denial or naïveté, but in alignment with my own experience, one moment at a time.

Trace the Roots of Your Illness

Let me be clear about this: No one really knows what causes cancer — not irrefutably, anyway. It strikes the young and the old, the rich and the poor, smokers and nonsmokers, juicers and fast-food junkies, vegans and meat eaters, the sad and the happy, the depressed and the joyous, the weak and the strong. It is seemingly indiscriminate and can't be connected to any one thing, including genetics. Even smoking can't be called a definitive cause of cancer because there are people who smoke who *don't* get cancer. That's why so many smokers take their chances, hoping to win that particular lottery, telling themselves cancer will likely pass them by.

The truest thing we can say about cancer is that there are contributory factors. There is significant evidence for many of those factors, including smoking. Some of the factors are the source of considerable disagreement and debate. For example, most qualified nutritionists and some more progressive oncologists (including several I have been fortunate enough to consult) are convinced that cancer feeds on sugar. Having craved sugar almost uncontrollably in the months leading up to my diagnosis, I sensed some truth in this for myself and I cut it from my diet immediately. I have even been prescribed Metformin, a drug for diabetes, by three unorthodox oncologists, to keep my blood sugar low. It is the only drug other than my tumor inhibitor that I take every day. However, my primary oncologist says there is no evidence to this effect, and encourages me to eat a balanced diet that can include chocolate and chips. There are even bowls of sweets placed next to the chemo chairs in the oncology unit at the hospital.

So what do I know? I am not a scientist, doctor or health practitioner of any kind. In fact, I paid such minimal attention to my health before I got the cancer diagnosis that I am still in wellness kindergarten. But — and this is a big but — I am a "terminal" cancer patient who has never felt more healthy, vital, nourished and self-accepting than I do today. I have taken radical responsibility for my body, in full consciousness that the odds of my surviving are stacked against me, and yet the odds of my *living* — fully, vibrantly, vehemently, gratefully *living* — are stacked in my favor as never before.

Huge hats off to the tumor-inhibiting drug I am taking, which has made a massive difference to my physical well-being. But that is not the only reason I feel so very alive. My aliveness is the result of a deep and penetrating investigation into all the ways I have clogged or undermined my energy, happiness, worthiness, creativity, passion, purpose, lovability, peacefulness and sheer joie de vivre. It is a consequence of unmasking the physical, environmental, psychological and spiritual factors that may have contributed to what I now see as a healing crisis: my cancer.

This has been a surprising exploration, one that really began many years ago. I have been working in the field of human development, mind-set transformation, and spiritual awakening for more than twenty years. I worked on myself consciously and effectively, creating a life I felt proud of and satisfied in. Between running a successful consulting business and leading dozens of transformational workshops, I have made a significant difference to thousands of lives. I married my soul mate when I turned forty and am the mother of a dazzling daughter whose arrival answered my deepest longing for a family of my own. I have a rich circle of close, authentic friendships with people committed to living consciously, generously and bravely in a world addicted to fear, self-interest and comfort. And I had found a spiritual path that shattered the inanimate religious model I grew up with and confirmed my deep-felt faith that it was God, not the devil, living in the details of my life. In many ways, I was awake, alert, and brimful with happiness when I learned I had cancer. I was awash with blessings.

And yet. My cancer has deep, long roots. It is a very slow-growing cancer that is rarely detected until it reaches stage four. My oncologist attributed my cancer to a faulty gene and estimated I had been living with it, unwittingly, for ten to fifteen years. For me, this meant the seeds had been sown in my teens and early twenties, maybe when I was even younger. I didn't just want to treat the symptoms, because that made no sense to me (focusing only on the symptoms explains why cancer grows back even after people go into remission). I knew there was more to this than a faulty gene, which I had no power to change. To give myself any hope of raising my daughter, I needed to address the other underlying "causes" of my condition. Like a weed, cancer needs to be pulled up at the root.

It took me many months to trace the possible roots of my cancer, both through online research and by working with different health practitioners who helped me find possible underlying causes. Some were more obvious than others — like teenage eating disorders that did long-term damage to my colon, and smoking in my late teens and twenties. Others were less obvious, like unexpressed grief, prolonged periods of loneliness, and poor lymph drainage from years of sleeping in my bra because I found it so uncomfortable to sleep without one. I mean, bra-wearing. Who knew? I also had gum disease for many years, which any good biological dentist will associate with cancer and recommend you get scanned for, but none of my dentists did. There is also increasing evidence of the connection between mercury fillings (a highly toxic heavy metal) and cancer. This is disputed by orthodox dentistry, as are the dangers of fluoride, but I have had my mercury fillings removed, regardless, and no longer use fluoride toothpaste.

Once you start identifying the contributory factors that may have led to your cancer, or may simply be exacerbating it, then you can begin to form a response. Some contributory factors are physical, some are environmental, emotional or psychological. It is very unlikely that you can definitively prove any of these factors caused your cancer, but you can follow your intuition about those that seem most pertinent. For example, you know your own history of eating, smoking and drinking. You know what environments you have lived in. You can find out if there is mold in your walls or strong electromagnetic radiation in your house. You can ask your doctor to test your blood for bacteria and parasites. It doesn't matter if you can prove these things led to your cancer. What matters is that you begin to identify as many *potential causes* as you can so you can form an integrated plan that addresses all possible factors. What matters is that you are weeding your garden, regardless of whether each change you make directly impacts your tumors. It is still likely to improve how you feel, behave, and live your life. My own attitude is that if it doesn't harm me and it serves my overall well-being, then I will do it. For me, the benefits of acting on this attitude have been immense.

Obviously, I can't identify your contributory factors for you. If you want to accelerate your inquiry, then you can download a free series of short videos about tracing emotional roots of cancer plus a "Trace the Roots of Your Cancer Chart" from my website (sophiesabbage.com/freebies), which lists all the contributory factors I have discovered in my research. These may help you begin to put the pieces of your own puzzle together.

4
KNOWING YOUR PURPOSE

A few months ago, a friend with cancer came for lunch with his wife. In 2013, he had been diagnosed with a choroidal melanoma at the back of his eye. It was unsuccessfully treated with radiotherapy before his eye was removed. Less than a year later, the cancer had spread to his liver and he was given six to twelve months to live. A doctor by profession, he is a very sensitive man who wears his power quietly and has participated in transformational human development workshops for many years. Indeed, I was privileged to lead the workshop he took following his diagnosis and to play a small part in helping him come to truly peaceful terms with his situation. I will never forget him standing in front of the group and telling them, "I am a loving, humble and honorable man and I will be missed when I am gone."

At the time, I was deeply moved to see his

self-acceptance in full bloom just as his body was shedding its last leaves, but I didn't fully comprehend the stand he had taken until I sat with him as a fellow cancer sufferer in my kitchen at home. While he enjoyed a cup of coffee, some cheese, and a cookie my daughter offered him, I stuck vigilantly to organic vegetables and herbal tea. At first, I interpreted this as simply our different choices in how we approached our illness. He was taking the orthodox medical route and I was taking an integrated route by adding a number of complementary treatments to my orthodox ones. He was a doctor, after all, so it made sense that he might be dubious about the choices I was making.

I didn't want to express my concern about the food he was eating, but his wife asked me questions about my diet and he showed genuine interest too. He encouraged me to go for it, to do all I could to give myself the best chance of survival.

"I would if I were you," he explained. "You are in your forties. You have a little girl you want to raise and be there for. You have so much of your life ahead of you. It's different for me, though. I've raised my children and I'm a grandfather now. I have lived a full and blessed life. I don't want to spend my remaining time fighting and denying myself simple pleasures. I want to spend it appreciating every moment and letting nature take its course. I welcome palliative care, but I'm not trying to reverse my lot here. I accept it. In fact, this is the most connecting, wondrous and exciting time of my life. Everything is clearer and sweeter and more beautiful. I wouldn't miss this for the world."

That's when I understood that his choices were different because his purpose was different. His primary treatment goal was palliative care and his purpose was to live out his days in gratitude for what was, is, and still could be. *Boom.* So clear and simple. If that were my purpose, I would be enjoying wine, cheese and sugar too. I would be enjoying everything I possibly could. He was so at peace. There was no fear, despair or burden of suffering. He was in a state of wonder, surrender and awe.

It was different for me. My goal was, and is, to find treatment that will put me in remission, even though I am told that isn't possible, because I want to raise my daughter into adulthood by doing everything I can to become healthy, vibrant and well.

At the same time, I am a realist. I am acutely aware of how long a shot this is, and that I need to be as prepared for death as I am for life. However, unlike my friend, I am not willing to have a *purpose* like his. I know the power of purpose and don't want to point my boat in that direction. I also know the power of cross-purposes and don't want to undermine what I am aiming for with confusing counter intentions. This is tricky stuff.

Purposes are different from goals. *Goals* are particular results or outcomes you are after, often very specific and time-based. *Purposes* are the underlying guiding intentions behind your goals, the "why" behind the "what." For example, you may have a goal to lose ten pounds in weight and a purpose to feel healthier, happier, and more at ease in your own skin. It is the purpose, not the goal, that will get you there — or not. If you believe you have to lose weight because you're too damn ugly and your partner will leave you if you don't, the chances are you will be devouring chocolate cookies by the second day of your diet. We need conscious, loving, heartfelt purposes to motivate us, not judgments and fearful consequences. Your goals are where you're heading. Your purpose is the rudder on your boat.

This is often missed when we're planning.

We define goals, timelines, actions and choices, but miss *intentions* — our reasons for doing and being, our inspiration. This is never more important than when you are facing a life-and-death situation. Your purpose will guide and determine all your choices, especially the ones that seem almost impossible to make. When you don't know what to do and there are no "right" or "wrong" answers you can refer to, your purpose will show you the way.

I needed to dig deep for a purpose that would underpin my heart's desire to far outrun my prognosis while being humble enough to accept that my cancer is deemed incurable. I needed to harness my will to live alongside my willingness to die, to truly and ultimately let Thy Will — not mine — be done.

My first oncologist assisted me in this exploration. Having told me my disease was systemic and irreversible, he declared his aim was to extend my time and give me a "good quality of life." Reasonable as that may sound, I was furious. How dare he decide what we were going to aim for without giving me a say in the matter? This was my life. *My* life. And whatever shit was currently hitting the fan, I would be the one to decide what to aim for. In particular, I was rattled by his offer of a "good quality of life." I wanted to scream, "NO! I want a full life . . . a long life . . . an exhaustive, unabridged, fulfilled life! I want to get well, damn it! I want to reverse this! I want a fucking cure!"

Later, I realized his words had cut deeper than my understandable refusal to accept what he was saying. For fifteen years I have run an extraordinary course called the More To Life weekend, cocreated by my mentor, Dr. K. Bradford Brown. Dr. Brown was a clinical psychologist, psychotherapist and theologian who studied directly under Carl Rogers, Viktor Frankl and Alan Watts, three major contributors to the theory and practice of psychology in the last century.

Dr. Brown's mission was to advance and modernize transformative learning, making it accessible to anyone who wanted to change their life while enabling people to walk a conscious, courageous and sacred path through an asleep, fearful and secular world. A true servant-leader who grew a cadre of other leaders, including me, to take his work forward, Dr. Brown resisted being in the limelight or being hailed as a guru. He steadfastly refused to write a book about his work, claiming that "understanding it is the booby prize," because what he taught could only transform through experience and practice. Some of his students think that decision was a mistake, because it made him so invisible in the human consciousness movement and limited the reach of his work. So, with his wife's permission, we are beginning to publish his teachings in books like this one.

The profound purpose of the More To Life weekend course was first written in 1984. I have shared it with participants in the opening session of many courses over the years, then delivered it consistently (with a money-back guarantee if I don't): *To awaken you with an experience of life that will radically enhance your ability to transform the quality of everything in your life.*

Suddenly, that "quality" was being reduced to managing pain, being made comfortable, and minimizing my physical suffering. That was the opposite of how I had regarded "quality of life" all those years. To me, having "a good quality of life" meant being liberated from comfort — which is the opposite of aliveness — as well as minimizing mental suffering caused by the false beliefs, unfounded fears and unverified forecasts of the future that burden our spirits and blind our vision. A "good quality of life" wasn't something for me to settle for but something to strive for. It was sacred and miraculous, the result of seeing light in the heart of darkness, truth in the kernel of deception, and joy in the reflection of despair. It was an opportunity for limitation and possibility to walk hand in hand.

Today, I am grateful to that oncologist for choosing the perfect words to remind me that my purpose with cancer is the same as my purpose with every challenge I have faced since I took the More To Life course myself nearly twenty-five years ago: *to let this experience awaken my mind, free my spirit and heal my life, whatever the ultimate outcome.*

From the moment I heard that doctor's words, cancer became my teacher, not my enemy; my healer, not my killer; my awakener, not my destroyer. It is the greatest opportunity I had ever been given to transform the quality of everything in my life.

ASSESS YOUR REALITY

In order to find your clear purpose on this journey, you first need to assess your medical situation as accurately as possible. Chapter Three, on understanding your disease, will help you to do this. You need to ask questions and gather as much data as you can — as *soon* as you can. You need to know where you stand, what the experts say about your condition, what treatments are on offer and what other protocols might be useful or relevant. However, you can assess the big picture quite quickly. You don't need every detail in order to connect with your purpose. I connected with mine after my very first meeting with an oncologist and "incurable" was all I needed to know. Similarly, it is important to find out how early they have detected your cancer and what stage it has reached. Stage one is a very different picture from stage four, and your response will differ accordingly.

You also need to assess your personal reality. How old are you? Do you have kids or no kids, a partner or spouse? Can you continue working or do you need to stop? Have you fulfilled your life's ambitions or are you just starting out? What is your support structure? What is your financial situation? What does your health and well-being mean to you at this time? These may seem like basic questions, but they are important.

My friend who came for lunch is a grandfather who has retired from his profession and feels very grateful for the life he has lived. So he is accepting palliative care and enjoying what time he has left. I am the mother of a five-year-old. I have a husband to whom I've been married a mere eight years. I have a vision for my life I have far from fulfilled. I am also the primary earner in my family and have not yet laid the groundwork for them to sustain our current lifestyle without my income. These facts don't change the other fact — that I have late-stage cancer. Every day, people are ripped from life without a moment's notice. Ultimately, we are not actually in control. However, this is the landscape of my life and as long as I have breath in my body, I want to account for these realities as best I can. They influence my choices and inform my purpose every day.

WHAT DO YOU REALLY WANT?

I grew up with a lie in my head that played like an old record over and over into adulthood: *I want never gets.* This lie is embedded in the fabric of our culture, at least in Britain, making it very difficult for thousands of children to admit what they really want, let alone *go for it.* I have run dozens of courses for intelligent, talented adults who literally don't know what they want because they believe it is selfish or futile to *want* things. Wanting alone doesn't create results, though sometimes we get what we want without effort. Wanting is the starting gate of living intentionally, of knowing what to aim for, and galvanizing energy in that direction. It is the birthplace of vision, without which there is no clear trajectory or favorable wind.

So here is the big question you need to answer when you learn you have cancer: *Do you want to live or die?* Seriously. You may think, "Of course I want to live! What a bloody stupid question! Why do you think I'm reading your book, you dimwit?!" And I say, gently, I get that. I really get that. *But.* When you look closely and completely honestly at how you have lived up to this point, were you 100 percent in, fully committed, fully present, fully here and fully, gloriously, gratefully alive? Have you neglected, undervalued or discounted yourself in significant or insidious ways? Have you abused your body or behaved self-destructively? Have you ever been seriously depressed or suicidal? Is there any part of you that has said *no* to your life, consciously or unconsciously, through your actions and behavior?

If so, I ask again: *Do you want to live or die?* Because this is it. This is the time you get to decide — once and for all. This is what cancer is asking you. This is a healing crisis, your body's last-ditch attempt to fight

117

for its life, perhaps even a plea for you to choose life over death with every fiber of your being. If your situation is anything like mine, that choice may not be enough to reverse your cancer and make you well again, but it will be your best shot at extending your days as long as possible and ending them with consciousness and wisdom instead of anger and defeat.

My friend the doctor chose life as surely as I did. In deciding to let nature take its course, he chose to live fully, joyously and gratefully in every moment he has left. He chooses life now . . . and now . . . and now . . . and, as I write, he has outlived his six-to-twelve-month prognosis and continues to savor the wind on his face, the wine in his glass, the touch of his wife's hand and the memories he hangs like daisy chains around the necks of his children, grandchildren and generations to come.

WHY DO YOU WANT IT?

Purpose is your soul's answer to *why?* It rises from your deepest values like a blue whale rising from the ocean. It is the place where your deepest longing meets the world's lack. It never begins with "I have to," "I ought to," or "I should." It begins with "I want to," "I choose to," "I'm willing

118

to" because . . . because . . . because . . .

It really helps to start with a statement like "I want" and then add "because" to the end of your want and take the sentence further, rather than asking *why* you want to do this. *Why* takes you into your head (intellect, logic, rationale) and *because* takes you into your heart (feeling, passion, truth). When I ask my daughter why she is sad, she doesn't know the answer, but when I say, "Darling, you feel sad because . . . ," she finds the answer easily.

You can start with one "because" and keep adding them until your intention gets deeper and deeper. "I want this because . . . and I want that because . . . and that matters to me because . . ." And you keep going . . . until something pops in your soul and you just know that's it, your purpose, essence, raison d'être.

Let me share a personal example (and note the shifting tenor and resonance of my language as the intentions deepen, line by line, and begin to express the content and substance of my soul):

I want to get well because . . .

I want to raise my daughter into adulthood, be there for her when life is challenging, pass on my wisdom to her and learn wisdom from her, witness her unfolding and be amazed, humbled and grateful for who she becomes.

I want to grow old with my husband, partner him in raising Gabriella, raise him up when he falls, give him space to relax in his old age, uphold his spirit and see him when he cannot see himself.

I want to keep working — to write, speak, teach, support, serve and make a difference, to fulfill my calling and inhabit my gifts without hiding them under a bushel, to play my part in human awakening and evolution, to transform and be transformed.

And I want all this because . . .

I care deeply about my family, friends and the world I live in.

I am perceptive, poetic, wise, witty and astute.

I am one of the brave ones, the truth-tellers, the burden-bearers, the empathic feelers of the world's sorrow, the broken-open vulnerable scholars of reality and of life.

I am half-lived, half-shaped, half-learned, half-blossomed.

I am still pregnant with longing.

The stories I have planted in the griefs and glories of my life are just now sprouting, willing and ready to be told.

And I want my griefs and glories to bloom because . . .

I want to *live.*

I want to *thrive.*

I want to be astonished by the "me" I will meet tomorrow.

I want to be implausibly generous and gorgeous.

I want to inhabit my holy humanity until my body hosts the Mystery instead of my disease.

I want to incorporate dying into my living and, if necessary, living into my dying.

I want to place my cancer journey at the altar of hope and possibility.

I want to be evidence of the power of authenticity and of faith in our darkest hours.

WHAT DO YOU CHOOSE TO DO?

From purpose flows choice. The resulting choices are specific actions you will commit to that express and align with your purpose (or purposes). In effect, this crafts a plan. I don't think I need to tell you how to do that, but I do encourage you to make it realistic and to share it with someone who can support you to keep your commitments — especially when you are fed up or feeling very ill.

In my situation, it was necessary to create Plan A and Plan B. Plan A flowed out of the above intentions. It was my "get well" plan. It included very practical medical choices like taking specific supplements, de-

121

toxing, changing my diet, consulting different practitioners, and raising funds for treatments abroad. It also included choices like creating my blog, which was my primary way of "evidencing the power of authenticity" — a bold decision to share my journey in a deeply vulnerable way. This book also ensued from that purpose. These were not choices I would have just thought of or reasoned myself into. In fact, when they arose I resisted them hard. I didn't want to expose myself when I felt so fallible, but my purpose was persistent — and it gave meaning to an otherwise traumatic and terrifying experience.

Plan B is my death plan. I won't share it in detail here because I don't want to give it more energy or power than it is due yet. I needed to have a death plan because my death was a probable early outcome. It remains, in the opinion of most of my doctors, the inevitable conclusion of my journey with cancer. From the moment I was told my cancer is incurable, my life was utterly changed. *Dying* is now an integral and intimate part of my *living.* It walks with me like a companion every day. I needed to embrace its presence and recognize that dying need not rob me of my purpose, that I could still be awakened and transformed by how I engage with that experience. Even the great wounds of my life could be healed before I died.

This was a revelation at the time, the beginning of my understanding that I could let cancer heal my life — *even if I couldn't heal my cancer.* I could forgive what I hadn't forgiven, repair relationships I had compromised or neglected, publish poetry I had concealed in private files on my computer, tell terrible jokes without worrying if anyone laughed or not, reconnect with schoolteachers who made me believe in myself when I hadn't before, replace the regrets of my life with gratitude for what I had realized along the way. I could die healed, just as I could live healed and go out transformed, just as I could survive transformed. The ultimate outcome is in God's hands, but this is entirely in my remit to do.

So, with all this in mind, I put my affairs in order. I updated my will and, with my brother's help (he was brave enough to broach this subject with me), made financial plans for my daughter's future. I also asked my sister to raise her if my husband dies before she turns eighteen. I choke just writing it. But Plan B was — and is — necessary.

Perhaps Plan B is necessary for all of us, whether we have cancer or not. Death, I am learning, is not the opposite of life or even just the end of life. It is the ebb of life's flow, a presence, not an absence, an intimate companion on life's journey, one that asks us to acknowledge its presence instead of denying it will someday find us. Doing so brings us closer to life rather than taking us further away. Living with cancer means seeing your own mortality in the mirror and choosing accordingly, as if every second counts.

Here is a simple but powerful five-step process to help you achieve what I have written about in this chapter:

The Purpose Process
1. *Results:* Write down the outcome(s) you want most in this situation. Be specific.
2. *Intentions:* Write down *why* you want these things. Use "because . . ." to keep deepening your intentions. "Because I want . . . because I am . . . because I . . ."
3. *Visualize:* Close your eyes and visualize yourself creating your desired outcome.
4. *Actions:* Write down all the choices, actions and commitments that flow from your deepest intentions.

5. *Support:* Choose at least one person to share this with and ask them to support you in fulfilling your commitments.

5
STABILIZING YOUR BODY

Before I could do most of the other things I share in this book, I needed to stabilize my body. I was in big trouble and had too little bandwidth for anything more than keeping myself alive. In order to stabilize, I needed to *understand my disease* to some extent, so I spent hours a day researching my condition, talking to medical consultants, and showing up for sessions with complementary practitioners. I had no idea what to do, so I started pulling together a team of experts who did.

The diagnostic phase of my journey took six full weeks and there were no medical interventions during that time. While waiting for a treatment plan to be determined, I felt extremely fragile and knew I needed to take whatever immediate action I could. But what?

My first instinct was to change my diet and I didn't want to wait until I had done my homework. I was fortunate to be supported by my dear friend Catherine Rolt during this time. As a long-term sufferer of Ehlers-Danlos syndrome who, nevertheless, radiates wellness, she is my role model for advocating your needs as a patient and thriving on pure spirit when your body is breaking down irretrievably. For several decades, she has disregarded many medical recommendations in favor of her own wisdom. She is a master practitioner of Chinese medicine and various other approaches to natural health and has a huge network of other master health practitioners, which she plugged me into like an electric circuit. She marched me straight to a nutritionist the day I got my first scan results, and I radically changed my diet that very day.

I didn't really know if it would make a difference, but what the nutritionist told me made sense, and I trusted Catherine deeply. I also trusted my intuition and this felt like the right thing to do. Most importantly, I needed to do something *for myself* instead of waiting for my oncologist to do something for me.

That decision was a pivotal psychological shift for me, a way of encouraging myself in the face of a seemingly insurmountable challenge and placing myself at cause in the situation instead of at its effect. To some extent, it didn't matter if my choices were sane or crazy (which some said they were). What mattered was *making the choices,* lifting my head above the parapet of despair and impossibility so I could take the next step . . . and the next step . . . and the next step. It was a return to driving my own karma, if you like. It seemed to me that if I let myself become a victim of cancer, cancer would sap my spirit as well as weaken my body.

In one fell swoop I stopped eating sugar, caffeine, dairy, wheat, gluten, alcohol, red meat and carbs. I even stopped eating fruit because of the sugar, which was the thing I missed the most. I expected it to be extremely difficult, but it wasn't. I guess my context was extreme enough to put the changes in perspective and motivate me almost effortlessly. After a lifetime of failed diets, struggling with food, loathing cooking (which I still do, actually), and staying stuck in the kindergarten level of healthy eating, I entered the advanced class in a single day. I don't think I've ever been so disciplined about anything. It was a no-brainer. My life was on the line.

I can't tell you categorically if eating this kind of diet will make a difference for you.

It is an area of significant controversy between natural and orthodox medicine. My doctors told me to eat a "balanced diet," yet they placed bowls of sweets in the chemo treatment rooms for their patients and pooh-poohed any suggestion that cancer thrives on sugar, a cause and effect that most qualified nutritionists and some of the more enlightened oncologists will confirm.

In my case, I listened to the nutritionists (having seen more than one), partly because what they said fitted my own experience of craving extreme amounts of sugar in the months prior to my diagnosis. I also considered that nutrition is a minuscule (bordering on nonexistent) part of medical training in this country, unlike in Mexico, where it is a major part of the curriculum. I simply didn't think my doctors were qualified to advise me on this matter.

Nor am I qualified to advise you. All I can do is share my own experiences and testify to their impact. In those first six weeks, I changed my diet and started taking a number of natural supplements. At the start, I was coughing hard for hours a day and felt breathless just walking up the stairs. By the end of that initial six-week period after my diagnosis, and before I began any other medical treatment, my coughing and breathlessness stopped. The dietary changes were that significant. Even now, when I am mourning cheese and red wine and telling myself diet can't be *that* important, so please, please, please can I break it, my husband reminds me of that remarkable turnaround in those early weeks. It didn't cure me, but changing my diet put me on the road to wellness and, perhaps more importantly, in the driver's seat of my journey. By the time I started receiving medical interventions, I was in charge.

That wasn't enough, though. I was still in acute pain from the large tumor on my C^3 vertebra, which was eating through the bone and threatening my spinal column. My oncologist, who said there was no point giving me radiotherapy for all my tumors because more would just spring up elsewhere, did recommend radiotherapy for my neck, to alleviate my pain and avert potential paralysis. I agreed. Another no-brainer. That was a painless but frightening and uncomfortable experience. A mask was made for me using a special kind of plastic heated in warm water so it becomes soft and pliable. This was molded to my face and then marks were made on it so they could accurately line up the radiotherapy machine for each treatment. It pinned my head to the bed to keep it completely still. It felt mildly suffocating, but it was tolerable and necessary, so I welcomed it as graciously as I could.

By that time, they had identified a genetic mutation in my cancer that qualified me for a chemo drug they hoped would inhibit my tumors. That meant taking a pill once a day instead of doing infusion chemotherapy, and my GP called this "a seriously lucky break." Normally, they would have done the radiotherapy first and started the drug a week later, but I was in Deep Shit City, so they recommended I do both at the same time. Again, no resistance. I was ready to take every "lucky break" I could get.

Those first few weeks were a long, dark night of the soul. I was told one of the side effects of the chemo drug would be a rash on my face, which seemed a small price to pay compared to relentless vomiting and going bald if I had done chemotherapy with traditional drugs. This was an understatement. After only six days, my face turned into a pepperoni pizza. It was swollen, burned, covered in acne, with chunks of skin peeling off like pith from an orange. At one point, my nurse spoke to my husband on the phone and tried to reassure him that a rash on the face was normal with this drug. Had I tried the cream they had given me?

"Rash?!" my husband exclaimed, furious at her implication that we were exaggerating the side effects. "She looks like someone took a blowtorch to her face!"

I also developed severe mucositis in my mouth and throat. This is a painful inflammation and ulceration of the mucous membranes, which have fast-growing cells like cancer and were therefore targeted indiscriminately by the drug. This was exacerbated by the radiation to my neck, which also burned my throat. I couldn't swallow food and could only manage little sips of water, which made the treatment unsustainable and untenable.

Worse than the pain was the fear. I couldn't live like this. I didn't want to leave the house. I had a small taste of what life must be like for people with severe scarring or deformity. People stared at my pizza face like I was a leper, and my self-esteem was soon hanging around my ankles like unelasticized socks. I needed to eat. I needed to like myself. It was all just too fucking much.

Two things saved the day. First, my daughter, who sees me with untainted eyes, looked at my pizza face and asked, "Does it hurt, Mummy? Shall I kiss it better?"

So I let my darling girl kiss my burning cheek and wipe away the two tears that silently escaped their ducts.

"Mummy," she said, throwing her arms around my neck, "you are beautiful and lovely — my special, special best friend."

And all was well again. The world righted itself. I remembered why I was doing this and what I wanted to live for. So I talked to my oncologist about the second thing that saved the day: adjusting the dosage. He said he hadn't ever seen such a severe reaction to this drug, so he first took me off it for two weeks, to let my damaged throat and skin recover (while reminding me that the drug was likely attacking my tumors as mercilessly as it had my face). Then we tried again. A few weeks later, my lips and nose were bleeding from mucositis, but my face and throat had healed. As had my sense of hope.

I had introduced some other treatments by then, mainly aimed at clearing my detox pathways (healing my poor digestive system and strengthening my kidneys and liver), and I think those initial treatments were the essential steps that stabilized my body. Although there is just as much to be said for a four-year-old girl reminding her mummy that love is a kiss on a disfigured face and beauty is a verb, not a noun.

When you are first diagnosed, your situation may not be as dire as mine was. Your body may be stable already, in which case you will have time to engage with the other parts of the program in this book. You may do this before or during your first phase of treatment. However, if you are anything like as unstable as I was, this stabilization of your body is one of your first ports of call. Only you can work out what this will involve, though your oncologist will be a primary guide to listen to during this time. But I advise you to also seek wider counsel and to take whatever additional steps feel right for you.

These steps will also depend on your purpose, which is worth getting very clear about right from the get-go, however ill you feel. Remember that your purpose is the rudder on your boat, so let it steer your choices. Stabilizing your body may mean doing all you can to check the spread of your cancer and control its symptoms. Equally, it could mean making palliative choices that reduce your pain and give you more time with your bucket list and loved ones. *You will know.* Either way, I hope the four steps I recommend in this chapter will help you navigate this part of your journey with a little more power and a little less pain.

As I write this, I am acutely aware that some people don't get much time at all, that even the choices offered in these pages may seem like a luxury if you are someone whose cancer has ravished your body beyond all repair. I wish I knew what to say to you. That I honor your courage, beauty and tenacity? That I can imagine the grief that will rise and fall like the night tide on the shore of your last days? That I can carve an enduring treasure chest for the memories you have made and the stories you have spun? No. My words are inadequate and my empathy incommensurate. My one hope is that, if this book finds its way to you, you may lift something from its pages that brings you some healing and peace.

If you are able to take action to stabilize your body, then I suggest the following:

Take Urgent Action

a) Listen to your oncologist and agree on the top-priority actions to take. This does not mean agreeing to the whole treatment plan that they may propose. It means identifying areas of immediate danger and attending to them immediately.

b) Seek second, third and fourth opinions if

you are able to, so you feel confident in the decisions you are making at this critical juncture. If possible, talk to an oncologist outside your own country, especially if you live in the U.S. or UK. Germany and Mexico are leaders in cancer care, but there are a number of reputable cancer clinics in other countries too.

c) Seek wider counsel from other kinds of health practitioners, like nutritionists, naturopaths, acupuncturists (I swear by these guys), and holistic dentists (there is increasing evidence of the connection between cancer and gum disease). Ask them to help you identify any urgent action you can take to stabilize your body. For example, I did colonic irrigation to get my dysfunctional colon working again, which made it easier to benefit from my new diet and to detox.

d) Seek support if you need it. I chose to change my diet, but I didn't know how to cook the kinds of meals I needed. This was one of the key areas where I asked for help. Some friends responded by stocking up my freezer with organic meals that followed my requirements to the letter. Their generosity lasted me nearly two months.

CHANGE YOUR DIET

You may want to do more research before making what can be a very challenging change in lifestyle, but I urge you to consider diet change very seriously. Dr. Contreras — who runs the Oasis of Hope Hospital in Mexico, which has been treating cancer patients for fifty years with notable comparative success — stated that the patients who follow their anti-cancer diet outlive their prognoses more often than the patients who don't. My diet combines his recommendations with others I have received from two nutritionists and from Dr. Dana Flavin, who, like Contreras, integrates orthodox oncology with other drugs and natural treatments.

These are the key things to remember:

- Cut sugar, gluten, wheat, alcohol, red meat and most carbs.
- Aim to be 80 percent vegan, but some chicken and fish is okay in moderation.
- Ideally, everything needs to be organic in order to avoid pesticides, so look into local sources of organic food. If you eat chicken or fish, organic is essential in order to avoid the growth hormones in farmed produce.
- Juicing is an incredibly fast way to mainline nutrients into your system and is also an

effective detox system. Juicing is different from blending, which includes retained fiber. Make your juices 80 percent vegetables and 20 percent fruit (green apples, blueberries, or raspberries). Carrots count as fruit because they are so sugary.

- Drink at least two liters of filtered water a day. If you buy bottled water, try to get glass bottles rather than plastic, which contain some contaminates. However, it is much cheaper to buy a good filter and make it last.

- Eat mainly alkaline foods. Cancer thrives in acidity so it is important to get your body as alkaline as possible. You can order alkaline litmus test paper to test your acidity levels (you pee on them). You can also find acid and alkaline food charts online.

Please note: The process of making your body alkaline takes patience, especially if you are taking pharmaceutical drugs, which also increase acidity. I have been working on this for nine months and am still too acidic, but I am improving slowly.

DETOX YOUR ENVIRONMENT

This is another proactive change you can make immediately. Some of these changes may seem unnecessary, but we live in a carcinogenic environment in many ways, and the more you can reduce toxins, the better. These are just a few ways you can minimize additional toxins entering your bloodstream and body:

- Get a good water filter for your drinking water.
- Get shower filters to remove chlorine and reduce water-soluble metals like lead, mercury, and copper.
- Minimize use of wireless technology by getting EMR (electromagnetic radiation) stoppers for your devices and to wear on your body somewhere. (I have one permanently tucked into my bra!) Switch off your Wi-Fi every night and, ideally, switch it off when you are traveling in the car as well. This is especially important if you have tumors in your brain. Never put your phone to your ear. Put it on speaker or use hands-free.
- Make sure there is no electromagnetic energy around your bed at night. Put phones, computers, and any electric devices, including alarm clocks and bedside lights, in another room.
- Banish microwaves from your life!

DETOX YOUR BODY

Like all the steps in this chapter, body detoxing is the subject for a book in its own right. There are plenty of books you can read on how to detox your body. I am no expert in this, but I know enough to say it needs to be a priority when you have cancer. These are the key things I want to highlight when stabilizing your body:

• Drink at least two liters of water every day.
• Detox through your skin with saunas, Epsom salt baths, castor oil packs, and skin brushing.
• Detox through your organs with colonic irrigation, coffee enemas, and an organic, mostly vegan diet. Plus, drink green juices!

You don't need to follow my recommendations in this chapter to the letter. They are intended as an overview only, and you will need to contact other experts or read other books for more information. I am simply sharing what has worked for me, in the hope that it will get you started and inspire you to find out what you can do for yourself. I am a cancer patient, not a health practitioner. I am also a cancer patient who qualified for a very effective tumor inhibitor, at least in the short term. I speak from my personal experience as well as the relatively limited but intensive research I have done since being diagnosed. I have confidence in these methods because they have made a difference to my healing and because I learned them from people who are master practitioners in their fields. As such, I encourage you to find practitioners of your own and work with them to formulate your initial urgent-action plan. Get some professionals behind you and alongside you. Don't just read books!

6
CLEARING YOUR MIND

CHOOSE YOUR ATTITUDE

As soon as I believed I was going to die, I started dying. No one actually said the "d-word," but it was the subtext of most of my interactions when I was first diagnosed. My cancer was "incurable," "irreversible," "late stage" and "systemic." There was no point operating on any of my tumors because new ones would simply pop up elsewhere. The statistics alone sounded my death knell. The only conclusion to draw was that I would be dead within a few months. Yet, two weeks earlier, I had felt normal, healthy and pain-free. In fact, I had been living with cancer unwittingly for at least a decade before it was detected and, while I recognize it had metastasized widely by that point, I still attended my first appointments feeling pain-free and *well*.

Awareness of my cancer changed everything. My mental landscape changed like a sudden storm from which I could find no shelter. A small creek of anxiety became a raging wall of water flooding my senses with foreboding and, try as I might, I could not shake the militant narrative of my inevitable demise. Within seventy-two hours of being told my cancer was "incurable," my life force began to dissolve like water decanted on sand. I had this strange sensation of rapid descent from a mountain I had been climbing all my life, having never reached the summit. It was as if a great wind had tossed me around the hillside and thrown me down the other side like a piece of discarded wreckage. My cough became relentless. My pain intensified. My energy thinned like drifting smoke. Before long, I was unable to pick up my daughter or even lie next to her simmering effervescence for more than a few minutes. Which was when my heart broke.

As part of me watched this happen, another part became conscious that I had begun to inhabit the story about terminal cancer without giving myself a chance to write my own version. I was screaming at myself from the margins, willing myself to walk off the page into another rendering of my destiny, convinced that saving my life began with shifting my perception that the sun was setting on my final days. This is what I had spent twenty years teaching people to do. I am very familiar with the power of the mind and its immense influence on what we feel, how we act, and whom we choose to become. I was well aware of the energetic messages our thoughts send to our cells — and the remarkable effects of mind-set transformation on our hearts, minds and spirits. I have seen the evidence too many times.

The powerful effect of beliefs on the body has long been borne out by the placebo effect, which was first described in medical literature in the 1780s. The placebo effect has been known to produce all manner of curative magic against various diseases. Today, we know that patients who are given empty injections or sugar pills, which they believe to contain medicine, can experience significant improvements in their health. In the case of cancer, neuroscientist Professor Andrew Newberg describes a cancer patient whose tumors "shrank when he was given an experimental drug, grew back when he learned that the drug was ineffective in other patients and shrank again when his doctor administered sterile water but said it was a more powerful version of the medication. The U.S. Food and Drug Administration ultimately declared the drug ineffective, and the patient died." Apparently, all that may be necessary for the placebo effect to kick in is for one part of the brain to take in data from the world and hand that information off to another part that controls a particular bodily function.

I have also recently discovered the "nocebo" effect, the exact opposite of the placebo effect, which is "literally lethal." A few years ago the *New England Journal of Medicine* showed the shocking results of a large study involving 500,000 patients being tested for cancer: if told their test was positive (not necessarily "terminal," just positive), there was a 29.6-fold increase in heart-related death within one week. In other words, the patient "is so convinced by the authority of the physician that the belief kills them."* Just as I am convinced I started dying when I believed I was going to die, so have I wondered how many people die of pure shock in a medical system that dares to predict our demise.

So how, when faced with a cancer diagnosis, do you get your brain to send healing messages to your body instead of fatal ones?

*This data was aquired from The Truth About Cancer documentary series by Ty Bollinger.

With all my years of experience in psychology, personal development and mind-set transformation, this shift was an Everest compared to any I had made before, almost beyond my reach. It was like mining my soul for diamonds. Yet I am convinced that the mental turnaround I eventually made was a vital precursor to the physical one I am now experiencing. I needed to make a quantum leap from "incurable" to "endurable," from "terminal" to "transformational," from "game over" to "game on."

This kind of mind-shift begins with understanding what my mentor, Dr. Brown, called the Principle of False Cause. This was rare knowledge when he started teaching it in the early 1980s but has since penetrated our wider consciousness, with different versions of it appearing in other teachings and methodologies. I have been teaching this model for more than twenty years and love its simplicity. The cultural misconception it dissolves is the idea that what we feel and how we behave is caused by external events. This is woven into the fabric of our language, dialogue, news reports and soap operas: *he made me angry; if that car hadn't cut me off on the road, I wouldn't be upset now; I have no confidence because my mum was mean to me as a child; I was unfaithful*

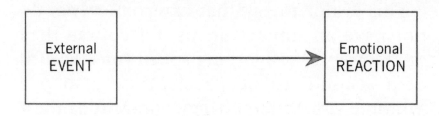

because my husband stopped noticing me; I feel scared because you are shouting at me. In other words, the belief that my experience is created by external circumstances. In actual fact, these external events trigger interpretive thinking, usually unconsciously, which is the true cause of our emotional reactions.

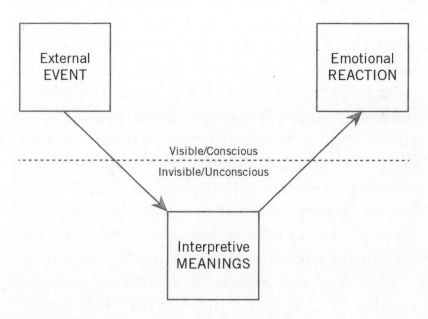

This is not to say that external events do not have an impact on us. Of course they do. However, at lightning speed (one-twelfth of a second, to be precise) we also put multiple dramatic and inaccurate meanings on the event itself. We perceive it through the filter of old belief systems. We make instant, uninformed judgments. We draw conclusions. We predict the future. We invent whole stories about others, the situation, and ourselves. We make shit up. Constantly. Our minds are meaning-making machines, relentlessly commenting on whatever is going on. This is known by some as "self-talk," "mental chatter," "mental stories," or "the ego," so you may be familiar with it. It's what Dr. Brown called "mind-talk," that voice in our heads that would love to run our lives if we let it. It does, in fact, run most people's lives most of the time. It is a powerful, persistent, controlling, calculating, crafty little sucker that needs to be brought to heel if you want to be in charge of your feelings, actions and choices. Especially when you have cancer or any other life-threatening illness.

The way we assign meaning to external events is the principle Viktor Frankl was talking about when he said, "The last of the human freedoms is to choose your own attitude in any given situation, to choose your own way." Between 1942 and 1945, Frankl labored in four different holocaust camps, including Auschwitz, while his parents, brother and pregnant wife perished. Based on his own experience and the experiences of others he treated later in his psychiatric practice, Frankl argues that we cannot avoid suffering, but we can choose how to find meaning in it and move forward with renewed purpose. We can also transform the meanings we assign to any given experience and thus transform our responses to it.

I witnessed this most poignantly some years ago when I was facilitating a leadership course for Mandela Rhodes Scholars on Robben Island. We were privileged to spend a week there, sleeping in converted prison cells and coaching bright young Africans in a context that both humbled and inspired them. One day, an ex-prisoner who had been a companion of Mandela's there for many years showed us around the prison and shared stories of his experiences. As a few students stood in Mandela's cell (we could fit only a few at a time), one of them, astonished by the stark reality he was witnessing, asked, "How did you survive in such a small space for so long?"

Our guide smiled for a moment before

responding, "Because the space wasn't small. It was *vast.* We were in Africa!"

I remember the tears rolling down our faces as we walked with him, dumbfounded, beginning to glimpse the remarkable perceptions that enabled those prisoners to lead a country to freedom from six-by-six-foot cells. This is the ultimate power we have as human beings. We cannot control what happens to us, but we can control how we perceive what happens and how we choose to respond. Or, as Maya Angelou so eloquently put it, "You may not control all the events that happen to you, but you can decide not to be reduced by them."

My own diagnosis called me to apply these principles as never before. I couldn't control the fact that I had stage four metastatic lung cancer, but I could decide not to be reduced by it. I could refuse to become simply a character in my limiting story about cancer and, instead, become ever more myself in response to cancer. *I could choose my attitude in this given situation. I could choose my own way.*

YES, BUT HOW?

Shifting your mind-set takes practice and experience. I have been teaching people to do this for many years and, once learned, it

150

becomes possible to apply the techniques to anything in your life without needing to rely on a coach, facilitator or therapist to get you there (though I continue to draw on strong emotional support in this situation, because it is acutely challenging and I'm not up for doing it alone). Perhaps the best way to give you a feel for it is to share how I shifted my own mind-set in relation to cancer. This includes sharing the specific steps of a powerful skill called the Clearing Process (summarized at the end of this chapter), which you can try out for yourself or learn to master with experienced support. You can find support from the information I've provided about courses and coaching in the supplement at the end of this book, called Support Systems.

RE-EXPERIENCE YOUR LIFESHOCKS
"Lifeshock" is a term Dr. Brown coined for certain external events. It refers to a *very specific moment in time when something happens that gets your attention,* when life shocks you with an event you weren't expecting. Lifeshocks can be positive or negative, welcome or unwelcome, big or small, obvious or subtle. They happen dozens of times a day, though it takes practice to notice them. Our minds are

constantly interpreting them, whether we're aware of it or not. We experience them through our senses — sight, smell, touch and sound — and they are more precise and particular than broad, significant events.

For example, having waited many years to have her, my daughter's birth — after several rounds of IVF — was one of the most positive and welcome events of my life. But that event was a tapestry of different lifeshocks woven together to create an awe-inspiring, life-changing experience. The one I remember most vividly was the moment the surgeon who had performed my caesarian section passed her over the screen, umbilical cord still attached, and placed her on my chest, which still had sensation even though my abdomen had been anesthetized. The moment I felt her wet skin, covered in goo and blood, touch my skin, I was overcome with gratitude and awe. I feel it again now, after writing that sentence. My awe is sealed in my memory of that event like a fresh spring I can tap into whenever I close my eyes to re-experience it.

Similarly, but not so positively, receiving my terminal cancer diagnosis has been one of the most momentous events of my life. Again, this experience is a synthesis of specific lifeshock moments that stand out to me:

- Diagnostician: "This mass is very suspicious" (looking at the scan, not at me).
- Diagnostician: "Don't become a patient, Mrs. Sabbage."
- Oncologist: "I'm afraid your cancer is incurable."
- Oncologist: "My main aim is to give you a good quality of life."
- Radiotherapist: "You have multiple tumors in your brain."
- Radiotherapist: "We need to radiate the whole brain as soon as possible."
- Radiotherapist: "It is possible your hair will never grow back."
- Radiotherapist: "The tumor on your C_3 is threatening your spinal column."
- Having applied for treatment with Dr. Muñoz (who apparently never turns cancer patients down), my husband, John, saying: "He won't take you, darling. He can't treat the brain."
- John: "How will I raise Gabriella without you?"
- Dad, on hearing the news: "My dear, dear child."
- Catherine: "It's a life sentence, Sophie, not a death sentence."

153

- My GP: "Lung cancer prognosis is very poor."
- The first time I coughed blood: seeing it land in the bathroom sink.
- Tripping on a London pavement and feeling pain ricochet down my spine.
- Trying to pick up Gabriella and not being able to hold her: seeing her fall back on her bottom when I dropped her.
- Gabriella: "Mummy, are you going to die?"

These are just some of the lifeshocks I remember from that time. Notice how specific they are (e.g., not just coughing blood, but seeing blood land in the sink). It is important to write them all down like this, with the specifics, even if you can only remember a few. As you do this, you may notice the same feelings surface that you felt at the time. This is because your emotions, and the unconscious mindtalk that caused them, are all locked together within the memory of that moment in your mind. By closing your eyes, taking some deep breaths and re-experiencing a lifeshock, you can literally unlock your unconscious thinking from that time.

This doesn't happen when you just remember a broad event. The mind will duck and dive to escape your pursuit, like a criminal on the run, determined not to get caught and confronted. By focusing on specific moments, you can expose your thinking much more easily and start to hear how you unconsciously interpreted what happened. You don't need to do this for every lifeshock. Just choose one that has the biggest emotional charge when you write it down and that will get you where you need to go. They all reveal similar mindtalk, which usually runs like a stuck record, repeating the same fears and beliefs over and over, whatever the situation. In this regard, all roads lead to Rome.

KILL YOUR KILLER BELIEFS

The next step is to write down everything you fear, think, believe and assume in relation to the lifeshock you are focusing on. Everything. In full sentences, exactly as you hear them. Unbridled and unedited. This is no time to be reasonable and controlled. You need to let your irrational voice speak. Give it permission. Blow its cover. If you go back to the lifeshock moment in your mind's eye and feel your feelings, you will likely start hearing your mindtalk very quickly. You may only hear a few sentences at first, but you can tune in to more by using "if that . . . then . . ." to see what else your mind has to say. For example, "If I've got cancer, then I'm going to die . . . and if I'm going to die, then I'm letting my family down . . . and if I'm letting my family down, then I've betrayed them . . . and if I've betrayed them, then I'm selfish and disloyal and they won't forgive me . . . and if they won't forgive me, then . . ." Notice how your mind wants to finish the sentence. That's how this works. You keep going until you can't hear any more mindtalk and you write it down, sentence by sentence, exactly as you hear it.

By putting all this on paper, you can then look at it objectively in the clear light of day and see it for what it is: *lies.* Well, mostly lies. There are facts and there are interpretations of facts, and it is essential to know the difference — perhaps even lifesaving to discern which is which.

We pile unnecessary suffering on top of natural suffering with our inaccurate, unsubstantiated and dramatized meanings that rob us of our clarity, creativity, self-respect and personal power. We usually do this without noticing or questioning the *nonsense* that blasts through our brains like tidal waves, clinging to our precious meanings like buoys in the ocean when we're shipwrecked and scared of drowning. We are swept away from reality by the stories we tell ourselves; then we wonder why we feel powerless and isolated and lost.

So here's the thing, the liberating, life-changing, gobsmackingly simple but truly transformational thing: Everything you think is verifiably *true, false,* or *you don't know.* Everything. And if you can harness this understanding to dismantle your stories, then rain will fall on your desert, and stars will blanket your darkened skies.

This process involves verifying each line of your mindtalk as *true, false,* or *I don't know* and then replacing false statements with true ones. This is different from:

- Replacing negative statements with positive ones: e.g., "I am the worst" to "I am the best," neither of which is true.
- Affirming beliefs in the hope that they will become true: e.g., "Money comes to me easily and abundantly," when, in fact, you are struggling to pay the bills.
- Turning beliefs around: e.g., "My mother is manipulative and selfish" to "I am manipulative and selfish," when, in fact, neither of those statements are fundamentally true about either of you (as in that's what you are at your core) — even if you have done selfish and manipulative things at times.

When I did this process on the lifeshock

of hearing the oncologist tell me, "My main aim is to give you a good quality of life," these were some of the beliefs I went on to verify:

I'm going to die soon. **Don't know.** I really don't know.

I can't bear this. **False.** I can bear this. I am bearing this.

I don't want a good quality of life. **False.** I do.

I want a long life, a full life. **True.**

I have to stay here for Gabriella. **False.** I want to, deeply, but don't have to and may not be able to.

I can't leave her. **False.** I can, even if I don't want to. And I may not have a choice.

It will devastate her. **Don't know.** She may feel great grief, but I don't know how she will deal with this. It may be the making of her as a person. I just don't know. But I do know she has amazing people in her life to help her through this.

I am her whole world. **False.** I am her mum, whom she loves hugely. I am a big part of her world, but her world is much bigger than me.

I'm her safe place. **False.** She does feel very safe with me, but I can't guarantee her safety, especially if I have terminal cancer.

It will be too hard for John. **False.** My

husband is incredibly strong. He will do what it takes to take care of our daughter and live a fulfilling life.

It's my fault. **False.** I have done some self-destructive things over the years, but this was caused by multiple factors and not one particular "fault."

I've wasted my life. **False.** I have had a full, blessed life of service. I have made a difference to many people. I have not fulfilled all my purposes or achieved all that I wanted, but I am proud of what I have created, how I have loved, and what I have given. I have also neglected things that matter to me, like writing, and I've hidden out when I wanted to be more visible. I would like the chance to correct those things.

I've betrayed my family. **False.** I am deeply loyal to my family and will do all I can to help them through this experience. I didn't promise them an easy ride. I promised them an authentic one. I promised to help us learn from everything that happens and do the best we can with what we have.

I'm irresponsible. **False.** I wish I had taken more responsibility for my health over the years. I wish I hadn't taken it for granted in the ways that I did. But I am responsible in many ways and response-able in this situation.

I'm selfish. **False.** No, no, no. I love, I care, I give, I feel, I empathize, I am deeply compassionate and generous. And, yes, sometimes I do selfish things. Having cancer is not one of them.

It's too late. **Don't know.** This is just the start of my journey. I don't know what I can do to turn this around or extend my life, but I will do everything I can.

It's terminal. **Don't know.** *Life* is terminal. I have stage four metastatic cancer. It is systemic. My oncologist can't reverse it, but we don't know how long I have or what is possible.

My time is up. **False.** It's not up until it's up.

My life is over. **False.** I am alive now. I am here now. My life goes on *now*.

I call this "killing your killer beliefs" because they can sap your energy and vitality as surely as your tumors can. By verifying your mindtalk in this way, you can lift the extra burdens of guilt, fear and self-recrimination that can choke your courage, creativity and compassion just when you need them most. Cancer creates a psychic space where lies can enter like bacteria and proliferate your disease. Cancer's stronghold is fear. It arrives, announces your death (often with a target date), and clamps itself to your ensuing panic like a baby to a billowing breast. This is part of what makes cancer so effective. It feeds on your conviction that your days are now numbered and the writing is on the wall. Your fear becomes its refuge and your stress its sustenance. It seems to thrive on resignation and despair.

In order to verify mindtalk effectively, it can really help to understand the difference between who you are and how you behave. *You are not your behavior.* You are you, and you behave how you behave. When my mentor, Dr. Brown, ran courses in prisons, he helped the prisoners understand the difference between "I am a criminal" and "I have committed crimes." The former is an absolute judgment that consigns that person to continue committing crimes in future because "that's who I am." The latter was a truth that enabled them to take full responsibility for their actions without their actions becoming their identity. The liberation those guys experienced from recognizing this difference was extraordinary. Some would go to their cells to weep with relief in private where they wouldn't lose face, finally able to see a way out of the hell they had created for themselves. Imagine the impact that might have on reoffending trends if more "criminals" realized this truth.

Verification is about being as truthful as you can. It is about taking responsibility for your behavior rather than writing yourself off because of your behavior — or letting yourself off the hook by affirming how great you always are. It is not about being positive or negative. It is about being *accurate.* For example, "I don't know" is a profoundly liberating accuracy to claim when your mind is predicting the future — which it *never, ever* knows. Nor does it know what other people are thinking (unless you ask, and even then we don't know for sure what they really believe). We just project our own thoughts onto other people and then tell ourselves, "He thinks I'm weak." If he hasn't said so, you don't know that. Even if he has, it isn't true anyway. Here are some important principles to remember when verifying:

- All statements about the future are *don't know.* You may think you know (based on the past). You may be convinced you know. You may argue that you do know until you're blue in the face, but *you don't know the future.* Ever.
- All generalizations are false; e.g. "I am selfish" (as in that is who I am) is false. "I did a selfish thing" (as in my behavior), in contrast, may be true.

162

- All "shoulds" and "have tos" are false. These can be tricky to see as false because they often seem reasonable, but they are *demands* vs. *choices*. For example, it is true that I *want to* be vigilant about my treatments, but false that I *have to.* It is true that I *choose* not to eat sugar, but false that I *shouldn't.*

Verifying can take some practice and is worth mastering with a coach if you see the potential value in it. You can get started now by choosing a cancer-related lifeshock and going to work on it. It may actually be a lifesaving thing to do. If I had believed everything that went through my head when I was diagnosed, I very much doubt I would be alive today. I was convinced I was going to die within a few months. I believed it was my fault and, therefore, I didn't deserve another shot at living. And I bought "incurable" as an irrefutable, cast-in-stone absolute — where the escarpment dropped away into the darkness and the wind blew out the stars. Fear, shame and regret damn near killed me before my doctors worked out a treatment plan, which I started six weeks after my first scan. During those six weeks, I flew through a long night of fear, delusion and obscuration until truths rolled out in my dark sky like landing lights on a runway, showing me the way back to reality and a path forward to possibility. Here are some of the truths that gave me hope:

- Cancer is a symptom of other underlying diseases that I can investigate.
- There is no cancer that has not been survived by someone.
- There are many terminal cancer cases that have gone into remission.
- "Terminal" is another word for mortal.
- I am not a statistic.
- I am not a victim.
- Cancer is a healing crisis.
- My attitude to cancer is awakening me.
- My attitude to cancer is transforming me.
- Cancer is forcing me to take radical responsibility for my health and well-being.
- I want to live.
- My life is worth saving.
- I have choices about my treatment plan.
- I am a person first, a patient second.
- I have cancer. Cancer does not have me.

That last one, "I have cancer, cancer does not have me," brought a game-changing shift to my perception and later became the title of my blog. It put me at cause in this situation instead of at cancer's effect, and from that point on, I got very creative. Whenever I'm down or slipping into despair, I come back to this truth to adjust my sails and spur me forward. And I do need to come back to it. I need to continue these processes, verify my own mindtalk regularly, because my mind gets at me regularly. It is an integrated part of my treatment plan.

MAKE CLEAR CHOICES

Once you have gone through the process of verifying your mindtalk, you can make some choices based on what's *true.* This is a shift from fear to love, separation to connection, reactivity to responsibility, powerlessness to creativity. In this book, I have shared many of the choices I've made — my Plan A and Plan B, my integrated treatment plan, my decision to write a blog about my journey, my e-mail to friends about how to help me, my willingness to let people love me through this instead of toughing it out, my decision to stop work while I focused on my wellness, making myself available to other people with cancer, even writing this book. Looking back over the past ten months, I see that this has probably been the most creative, productive and transformative time of my life.

I can't advise you about what specific choices to make. I can confirm that you won't find them when your mindtalk is running the show. They will emerge when you raise the blinds of self-deception. Some of them may surprise you. Seeing them will feel like arriving in a clearing after wading through a thick swamp on a rainy day and feeling the sun on your face again. You may choose conventional treatments or alternative treatments or both. You may choose to share your journey with a few trusted friends or shout it from the rooftops to complete strangers. You may choose to manage your pain or experience your pain. You may choose to drink wine or abstain from wine. You may choose to battle your cancer or befriend your cancer. You may choose to fight or surrender, to live as long you can or die as peacefully as you can. What matters is the *choosing,* the galvanizing of your will and the nurturing of your willingness to catch this curveball and run with it through your days.

In August 2015, my friend with choroidal melanoma (whom I wrote about in Chapter Four) died. He was very thin when he passed, but very peaceful and accepting. One of his last requests was for his daughter to read the loving messages left by his friends on the Caring Bridge website. His wife responded online to those messages by sharing this excerpt from David Whyte's writings:

*The ultimate touchstone of friendship is
not improvement, neither of the other nor
of the self, the ultimate touchstone is witness, the privilege of having been seen by
someone and the equal privilege of being
granted the sight of the essence of another, to have walked with them and to
have believed in them, and sometimes just
to have accompanied them for however
brief a span, on a journey impossible to
accomplish alone.*

My friend's choices, so different from
mine, inspire me daily and remind me that
for all my choosing, I am not ultimately in
control. None of us are. All we can do is
lean in to the realities that reveal themselves
moment by moment on this journey with
cancer. We can meet what comes today
without predetermining tomorrow, and take
the next step, and the next step, from *here,*
wherever *here* is now. That pilgrimage, from
the future to the present, is one of cancer's
great gifts to me, a bridge I have spent
decades trying to cross, always stumbling
before I reached the other side to plant my
feet firmly in the *now.* It is a pilgrimage
many people never begin or even consider
until faced with their own mortality and the
ever-present possibility that tomorrow may

not come.

When the tide turns for me and I know in my bones that I am dying, I pray to choose death as unequivocally as I am currently choosing life. We can meet our dying with a "yes" as affirmative as our "yes" to living, with a willing engagement instead of a fearful resistance, with a **choice.** We can be killed by cancer, as passive victims of a grim reaping, or we can die actively, choosing cancer's meaning for ourselves, as my dear friend did, slipping through love's curtains consciously, empowered, inspirited and bathed in wonder to the last.

GET EMOTIONAL SUPPORT

If there was ever a time to get psychological, emotional and spiritual support, it is now. I have met many cancer patients who say they were emotionally shut down until they got cancer and now they can't stop crying, as if the dam inside broke. Aside from the importance of tracking the emotional roots of your cancer, emotional support is important because it also provides you with a safe place to take your angers, fears and sorrows as this process unfolds.

You can find this kind of support in different forms: support groups, coaches, therapists, counselors, workshop facilitators and spiritual guides. You are likely to be more drawn to one of these than the others, or you may want to combine different approaches. You may also want to learn more about the skills I write about in this book. In the supplement at the end of this book, I have included information about how to begin that learning. Support is available if you want it. All you need to do is reach out.

I needed to reach out for support, even though I am emotionally intelligent and expressive, and have these skills in my hands. I feel my feelings easily, know how to shift them and teach others to do the same. Yet having cancer still begged the question, "Where am I emotionally blocked and *dis-eased*?" This is an ongoing inquiry, much of which I share in this book (especially in Chapter Eight).

The length and breadth of this particular journey is yet to be told because it is still unfolding in ways I don't yet have words for. I have found a remarkable therapist who is accompanying me on a spiritual odyssey. I hope to write another book about that part of the journey, once I've assimilated these sacred truths in a way I feel confident enough to share. I am in no doubt that this spiritual dimension to my experience with cancer is the most healing, restorative and liberating of all. It is how I work through the terror that still wakes me up in the night and tortures me until morning. It is how I reach down into my childhood and squeeze its leftover hurts from my eyes. It is how I remember my value and why my life is worth living. It is how cancer becomes my healer and, slowly but surely, reveals its divine purpose to me. It is how I feel blessed, not cursed, by the presence of this disease in my too-often forgotten body, and how I arrive on the shore that the very ocean of life calls home.

This is a summary of the process I have described in detail in this chapter. Dr. Brown designed it in 1984 when he co-founded an educational program called The Life Training, now called More To Life, with Dr. Roy Whitten. This global program aims to contribute to the transformation of the world, one person at a time, by equipping people to become their best, most authentic, most compassionate and creative selves. After fifteen years, I am still a senior trainer with this organization. I also spent twenty years teaching these processes in diverse organizations through the company I created with Dr. Brown and a visionary woman named Janet Jones.

THE CLEARING PROCESS

1. Re-experience the lifeshock and feel your feelings.
2. Write down your mindtalk.
3. Verify each line of your mindtalk as *true, false* or *I don't know.*
4. For each false statement or *I don't know* write down what *is* true.
5. *Choose* what to do and how to be.
6. Visualize yourself doing it and being it.

© K. Bradford Brown, PhD, 1984

7
DIRECTING YOUR TREATMENT

YOU ARE IN CHARGE

In the first few weeks following my diagnosis, I was flooded with opinions and advice — not just from my doctors and alternative health practitioners, but also from friends and family who had experienced cancer themselves, knew someone else who had experienced cancer or just knew stuff about healthy living that seemed to have passed me by. I was grateful for that because I have used much of that advice, and some of it got me started when I had no idea where to begin. At the same time, I found it overwhelming. Some of the information was contradictory, much was hard to compute when I was dazed with shock, and occasionally it was downright patronizing. Worst of all was being regaled with stories about someone or other with cancer who had done this or that and recovered — only to realize that the patient in question had had single-

172

sited, early-stage tumors that bore little resemblance to my multi-sited, late-stage, systemic disease. My spirit would lift like a bird taking flight, then come crashing back to earth with a thud. These were well-meant advice misfires from loving people who simply couldn't imagine what it was like to live in my skin. And, suddenly, my skin was the loneliest place in the world.

One of the few people who didn't do that was my friend Catherine. She called me every day, went with me to appointments, and listened, listened, listened to my despair. She was more qualified than most to advise me — having come through cancer twice herself, in addition to having lived with EDS all her life — but she didn't offer advice. At first, she withheld her counsel even when I asked, instead saying the same thing to me over and over: "Sophie, you are in charge. You are your own best healer. You will know what your body needs. The wisdom you need to listen to is your own."

I had a sense she was right, but I felt so out of my depth in this arena that it was hard to trust my instincts over the recommendations of highly experienced medical professionals. The turning point came when I was prescribed steroids for the metastases peppering my brain and was told that my whole brain needed to be radiated because there were too many tumors to target individually. Naturally, I felt very resistant to both prospects, but fear-based resistance and truth-based intuition are poles apart. The challenge was in recognizing the difference.

In my case, I believed that the steroids were unnecessary and I suspected they were potentially harmful. First, they increase blood sugar and I didn't want that to happen when I had worked so hard to cut sugar from my diet. Second, they can interfere with sleep and the body does most of its healing when we are sleeping. Third, my oncologist had warned me that I would gain weight as a side effect and I didn't want that, either. I still hadn't returned to my pre-pregnancy size or fully recovered from the effects of IVF five years previously. I was already crawling through a very dark tunnel of despair and the last thing I needed was another threat to my self-esteem or the prospect of feeling even more uncomfortable in my diseased body than I already felt. So I told my doctor I wasn't willing to take the steroids.

He was quite concerned at first, but my explanations also made sense to him. My *no* wasn't ignorance, and I was willing to listen to his perspective. His main concern was that I would get severe headaches from the tumors and possibly have some seizures, which seemed completely valid and equally concerning to me. So we negotiated. I asked him to respect my decision about this but promised to reconsider if I started getting headaches and to actually take the steroids if I had a seizure — at which point we had a deal. It was the first of many such negotiations to come.

The second such challenge came hot on the heels of the first. I was extremely reluctant to have radiotherapy on my entire brain, even though I was acutely aware that my tumors were already compromising my eyesight and cognitive functioning. This was as tough a call as I was ever going to make, it seemed. It is notoriously difficult to find drugs that can penetrate the blood barrier in the brain, but I first wanted to see what effect my chemo drug would have before agreeing to radiotherapy and to explore alternative treatments at the same time. I was aware that Dr. Dana Flavin, with whom I had already consulted, had gotten rid of brain metastases in patients with breast cancer using natural supplements. Later, when I e-mailed her to ask if she could stop them frying my brain, she e-mailed me straight back: "Yes. I can. Boswellia Serratta and Berberin. 800mg three times a day."

That was all her message said. So I ordered those natural supplements immediately and I've been taking them ever since. Again, my oncologist agreed to my request to delay the radiotherapy because he believed there was merit in seeing if the drug I was about to start taking would make a difference. In turn, I promised to contact him if there was any worsening of my condition. This is very important to emphasize here. I was not acting in ignorance or defiance when I made those choices. Nor was I following an intuitive hunch without any supporting data or well-founded rationale to back it up. I was not acting against my doctor's recommendations because I was scared but because I was willing to respect my own wisdom. I was also willing to respect his.

It was a dialogue between us, not a conflict. It was essential that I listened to his guidance and was transparent with him about my choices. That way we were able to work out my treatment together and replace the prevalent top-down relationship between doctor and patient with a truly collaborative partnership that embodies patient-centered care. That was how I began to take charge of my treatment.

With regard to my brain, I believe that the combined effects of my chemo drug and natural supplements (plus a homeopathic dose of divine intervention) have made a big difference. Of course, I don't actually know. I've created such a gumbo of treatments, it's impossible to know where efficacy begins and the placebo effect ends. But this is of little concern to me as long as progress is being made and no harm is being done. What is of most concern is that I am directing my own treatment with as much information and intuition as I can muster, that I have claimed some semblance of power in the face of powerlessness, and that I can drink the sweet, seasoned wine of another life-drenched day until gratitude bleeds through the other side of fear and sorrow and dismay. What matters is the fact that five months after my original scan, my brain was tumor-free.

Making those decisions about my brain was a quantum leap forward in taking charge and learning to direct my own treatment. From that point on, I was ready to do everything I could to live as well as I could for as long as I could and — when my options were genuinely exhausted — to die as well as I could too. I don't mean live "comfortably" as in sedated and pain-free, numbed-out from the fear and horror of my premature demise. And I don't mean staying alive at any cost, following the "whatever it takes" doctrine that emerged from the success of medical technology and burgeoned into the expectations of patients and the demands of their loved ones. I mean to *live well* — vibrantly, consciously, taking my place in the story, fully engaging with what is happening to me, planting my heart in the people I love, grieving the closely guarded desires I had for my future, and remaining the author of my destiny, even in the face of my unassailable loss of control.

When I ask her to, these days, Catherine advises me. Over time, she has seen my own sense of authority grow and strengthen as I increasingly trust my intuition and discernment, and she sees that I am becoming my own best healer. So she is now willing to throw her extremely valuable insight into the mix because she knows I will do what I choose and not what I'm told. In this regard, the way she encouraged me to heed my own wisdom, she probably saved my life.

INTEGRATING TREATMENTS
From early on, I knew I wanted to take an integrated treatment path by combining

orthodox, synthetic treatments with complementary, natural ones. It seemed to me there was significant merit in both approaches and plenty of evidence to support that view. I saw no reason to choose between them and so I went about gathering a diverse group of practitioners to support me in my quest to "live well" (and, frankly, to *get* well, if there was even the slightest chance I could pull that off).

Before long, I had pulled together quite a team: oncologist, radiotherapist, nutritionist, naturopath, acupuncturist, colonic irrigator, lymph drainage masseuse, and some "integrative" oncologists abroad. Friends and family rallied around to raise funds for my treatments from this eclectic group of health experts and I did considerable research to choose wisely the practices I believed could make the most difference. Each of these practitioners has proved exceptional both in their field of expertise and in the depth of their care for me as a patient, for which I am deeply grateful.

Yet, perhaps naïvely, I expected everyone to bat for the same team in service of a single purpose — my well-being — and to collaborate willingly and enthusiastically on my behalf. Not literally, of course. I didn't imagine they would all be on the phone to each other, but I did envision they could be respectful and supportive of each other's contributions to my case. Instead, I found myself caught in the cross fire of a great divide: orthodox versus complementary, synthetic versus natural, conventional versus alternative. Natural practitioners berate the slash-it, burn-it, poison-it approach, while the doctors and oncologists caution me against anything that isn't rigorously (and expensively) evidenced and approved by the regulators. The two worlds are so positioned against each other that the patient is often left to figure it out alone and try to integrate the opposing views about their treatment.

Their positions aren't personal; they're evidence of a divide that's systemic. There is a mutual discounting that pervades these two paradigms and some of the discounting is with good reason. There probably are some complementary "quacks" out there who do a great injustice to the many practitioners who are highly trained and serve patients with real integrity. And the pharmaceutical industry has a lot to answer for in its tendency toward squashing, suppressing and bullying people who come up with alternative solutions. I don't need to harp on about this, but it really is a scandalous catalogue of putting profit before patient

care. As patients, we need to have considerable presence of mind and no small amount
of courage to forge the best possible path of
healing through this dense jungle of conten-
tion, self-righteousness and closed-
mindedness.

On one hand, my doctors raise judgmental
eyebrows about my strict diet and caution
me about alternative treatments I tell them
about, though I have learned to be selective
in what I inform them of to spare myself
the lectures. On the other hand, some of
my natural practitioners counsel me to
avoid chemotherapy and radiation like the
plague, because it is as likely to kill me as
my cancer. While I acknowledge some
compelling evidence to that effect, it is
easier to refuse chemotherapy and radiation
when your body isn't already riddled with
tumors that are sapping your life force and
causing you considerable distress.

It is not fun playing piggy-in-the-middle
when your life is on the line. I don't want to
be warned off what the other side is offering, nor be admonished for accepting it. I
don't want to hide what I'm really up to
from my doctors for fear of paternalistic, if
well-intended, warnings about alternative
treatments they are rarely qualified to comment on. And I don't want to be judged by

181

the purist natural healers for embracing what the Big Bad Pharma has to offer me.

I want to be transparent with everyone involved. I want to arch my diseased body into a bridge where they can meet in the middle and shake hands, with my well-being in mind. I want both sides to abandon their conceits and join me in the darkened corner of the world where I find myself. I want curiosity, inquiry, collaboration and a circuit of mutual respect in which serving the patient is their highest and noblest purpose. I want them to be bigger than themselves.

Fortunately, there *are* some doctors and health practitioners who really get it. For example, my marvelous acupuncturist and dispenser of truly disgusting but surprisingly effective Chinese herbs put it beautifully when he said, "You have terrorists in your house, Sophie. The chemo and radiation are the SAS, there to take 'em out. The rest of us are taking care of the citizens, the land and the building structure, which are so often destroyed by chemo. It's the best kind of teamwork."

Hearing that statement halved my stress levels and restored me from a taut piece of rope engaged in a systemic tug of war to a human being with cancer who is reaching for the silver crest of stars in a foreboding night sky. These are the kind of people you want on your team, the ones who support your choices instead of judging them, who see you as a person more than a patient, the driver and not the passenger on this ride.

UNDER THE RADAR

In the UK and the U.S., one of the big challenges for cancer patients is the tight regulation applied to potential treatments. In the U.S., Federal Drug Administration approval is required for treatments. On this side of the pond, approval is required from our FDA equivalent, NICE (the National Institute for Health and Care Excellence). There are some excellent reasons for placing controls on pharmaceutical distribution, but there are also some ludicrous limitations. For example, I go to a clinic in Kent for lymph drainage massage and colonic irrigation. The woman who owns it used to run a clinic that offered high doses of Vitamin C and ozone therapy, treatments I now travel to Mexico to receive, but she had to shut down her business after intense pressure from the media and regulators. She tells me she can't run the risk of offering those treatments anymore and can't even use the word "healing" to describe her services to customers in her marketing materials or her website.

One of the reasons so many cancer patients travel to Mexico for treatment is that the laws there allow them to offer cancer treatments that have been approved by any country in the world, not just their own. This gives them far greater room to offer a wider range of services. In addition, natural medicine and nutrition are a core part of medical training in Mexico, so Mexican doctors are able to integrate natural and synthetic remedies far more effectively than doctors in other countries.

While I welcome the treatments I have received in Mexico, it is a source of considerable frustration that it is so damn difficult, and in some cases impossible, to access those cancer protocols here in the UK. I have needed to raise a lot of money to go abroad for them and dearly wish I didn't have to. Interestingly, I am now plugged into a semi-underground network through which I have been able to access some treatments in the UK, but it isn't easy. I have met fully qualified GPs as well as highly experienced health practitioners who have to fly under the radar in order to provide these services.

This puts even more of an onus on you, the patient, to navigate your way through the maze and make wise choices. Due diligence is needed in researching any protocols and practitioners you engage with, but it can feel lonely and frightening to do all this while you are gravely ill. The risks you are willing to take will likely depend on how ill you are. Because I have been diagnosed with cancer at stage four, I have been willing to push the boat out pretty far. I'm not up for doing anything dangerous, but I would like to engage my oncologist to experiment more on my behalf. I would prefer not to have to coordinate and figure out so much for myself. Sadly, his hands are tied by legislation that prevents him from doing so even if he would like to.

As I write, Lord Maurice Saatchi, whose wife died of cancer, is working hard to change this situation by proposing the Medical Innovation Bill (now called the Access to Medical Treatments Bill), which would allow doctors to provide new and innovative treatments to terminally ill patients. Unusual for a private member's bill, he got it through the House of Lords in 2014, had a major national newspaper backing his cause and won considerable support in the country. However, it was then blocked in the House of Commons shortly before the May General Election in 2015 by the then health minister, Norman Lamb, on the basis that "some highly vulnerable people, desperate for a chance of recovery or remission, could be easy prey for exploitation by the few unscrupulous practitioners who peddle false hope." While I don't doubt that there are some exploitative clinics and unscrupulous practitioners who take advantage of people's vulnerability and fear, it seemed to me that the notion of my vulnerability was also being used to take away my power to decide for myself, and to score political points and justify a medical perspective that too easily discounts valid treatments that don't conform to conventional paradigms.

The second argument against the bill was "ensuring patient safety." I found it cruelly ironic to be denied the opportunity of greater innovation in the name of preserving my safety. Safety from what? The certain death I am already facing? The chance that I might die of something less predictable than the reliably fatal disease I already have? The peace of mind I might be afforded by going out knowing I pooled all my creativity to stay as long as I could, even while my doctors picked their creative toenails before finally conceding they could do no more? What, pray tell, safety from *what*?

I don't know what will happen to the bill and, truthfully, don't hold out much hope that it will pass into law. It will likely be booted out or diluted beyond recognition, and terminally ill patients will be left scrambling for options. As one of those patients wanting to access unapproved treatments, I have had to join an underground movement of cancer warriors who share vital information and help each other navigate a network of brave ass-on-the-line practitioners, including doctors and nurses, who are engaged in covert operations to save lives. It doesn't need to be this way. But it is.

This bill and this issue matter deeply because there are too many patients, like me, who are also trying to navigate their own healing through the labyrinth of restrictive legislation, amid conflicting views and a dearth of collaborations between cancer care practitioners. I have undertaken to move from one practitioner to another, gather a wealth of information from each of them, assess it and put it all together in my own integrated treatment plan. I've been able to share this plan with a few medical professionals, to assure myself that I'm not contraindicating different treatments or doing anything that could undermine the efficacy of my primary protocols. I have not been naïve. I believe my current wellness testifies to my treatment choices so far. But this process hasn't been easy. In fact, it has been a demanding endeavor and a full-time job. It has also required me to have more faith in myself than in any of the people around me — which has been yet another of cancer's unexpected contributions to the healing of my life.

FOUR KEY NAVIGATION INSTRUMENTS

1. Listening to the Experts

First and foremost is to remember that you are a patient, not a doctor (unless you actually are one). As such, it is essential that you find out everything you can from your health practitioners before making any big decisions. Being autonomous in your decision making does not mean being arrogant or going solo. It means self-government, self-determination and the freedom to make your own choices. All too often, patients give up autonomy when diagnosed with a serious illness. Fear can make you passive. It can paralyze your capacity to make significant decisions and it can profoundly undermine your self-confidence. Equally, it can make you aggressive, defensive and unwilling to listen to other points of view. Neither of those stances will get you where you want or need to go.

True autonomy comes from listening first and choosing second. Find out what the experts know and take it seriously, but don't automatically do what they say. Be highly respectful without handing over your power. Create a context of partnership, not of obedience or opposition. Take a notebook with you to your consultations so you can write everything down. If you have a companion to accompany you, ask them to do it for you so you can concentrate on *listening.*

When you're scared or distressed, your mind will interfere with its internal chatter, blank out what is being said or miss crucial bits of information. So I recommend repeating back what you hear, either in summary or word for word, as necessary, to assure yourself that you have heard the information accurately. This is a skill called "playback" that I have been teaching for many years in different contexts. It is a very powerful and effective thing to do, especially in situations of conflict or crisis. I often use it with my daughter when she is upset or angry, partly so I know I've really heard her and partly so *she* knows I've really heard her. "So you wanted a pink balloon and I got you a green balloon and it just isn't the same because you're a princess, not a frog?

189

Got it. Well, no wonder you're so angry with me." This is a far cry from the "Don't be so silly" approach and restores harmony a good deal quicker.

I always use playback when I am confused, scared or distressed in consultations with my doctor or oncologist. "So, you're saying I have tumors in the lining of my brain *and* in the tissue of my brain . . . that there are too many to count, let alone target with radiation individually? You want me to take steroids to reduce the swelling and control the symptoms? And you want to start radio-therapy on my brain as soon as possible? Is that what you're telling me?"

I have done this so many times I've lost count. I always need to be sure I have understood what I'm being told — fully and in detail — without blocking something out just because I don't want to hear it. Above all, I want to educate myself about my disease so that my comprehension is as comprehensive as possible. My intuition can't fly in the dark. It needs some lights, signals and weather warnings to find its way.

2. Using Your Intuitive Compass
Once you have listened to others, it is time to listen to yourself. Intuition is the ability to know something instinctively, feeling it in

your bones without the need for conscious reasoning. Indeed, conscious reasoning usually gets in the way of intuition, drowning it out and causing us to question, doubt or disregard it. If you are trying to figure it out, you are not intuiting. If you are rationalizing both sides of the argument, you are not intuiting. "Reasoning" is learning from without. "Intuition" is learning from within. Intuition is an internal compass, the voice of your spirit, directing you to the truth. I think of it as the eyes of my soul.

Sadly, most of us are not taught to use intuition. Indeed, we are often taught to shrug it off or disregard it as illogical and untrustworthy. Albert Einstein said, "The intuitive mind is a sacred gift and the rational mind is a faithful servant. We have created a society that honors the servant and has forgotten the gift." If this rings true for you, and you have cancer, rest assured that your discomfort with trusting your instincts is based on centuries of cultural prejudice. It is time to remember and reclaim this gift.

I am suggesting that you use reasoning as well as intuition. That's why I put "listening to the experts" first as a key navigational instrument. It's very helpful to gather data, inform and educate yourself, then use your intuition to guide your choices. Equally, you may have a hunch about something and, not trusting it, want to do more research before making an important medical decision. When my gut said *no* to taking steroids, I was already aware that they affect weight and sleep, but I later found out they also increase blood sugar. That information was what I needed to confirm my instinct, which was hard to trust in the face of convincing medical advice to the contrary.

Your intuition is a muscle that needs exercise. If it is already strong, this is the time to flex it. If it isn't, this is the time to take it to the gym. In my experience, my intuition is wonderfully reliable even when my body is weak and my mind is tired, but fear silences it. Sometimes, I am in too much of a panic to feel any instinctive sense about anything. If that's what you're experiencing, it is time to *clear your mind* and use the tools from Chapter Six. When your mind is quiet, your intuition is set free.

I recommend these additional ways of supporting and strengthening your intuition:

1. Keep a journal about your journey with cancer. Write down all your thoughts and feelings without editing them. This helps the unconscious mind to open up. Intui-

tive wisdom will sometimes just surface on the page and show you the way.

2. Engage a trusted friend, life coach or therapist to help you listen to your intuition and see with your soul. Sometimes you just need to empty your cluttered head by talking it all out to another human being. Then, in the clearing, you suddenly "know" what to do. I do this with my husband, my friend Catherine and my therapist at different times. They are my emotional and spiritual lifeguards.

3. If you want to master the skills in this book, I invite you to explore my website (sophiesabbage.com/events), where you will find information about the products and courses I offer, both for cancer patients and anyone seeking to transform their lives.

4. Find a quiet, solitary place to sit in silence or meditate. Go inside yourself and let your feelings flow freely or find a piece of music, literature, or a treasured object to connect with. Learn to use your breath consciously, breathing in through your nose, down into your belly, and then out through your mouth, like you're blowing out a candle. When you're concentrating on breath, the mind quiets and intuitive senses expand.

If you love art, nature, music or literature, then draw on these resources too. For me, words are containers full of life and healing. Reading someone else's cancer story, or lying in an Epsom salts bath reading poetry by the American poet and Pulitzer Prize winner Mary Oliver or by the thirteenth-century Sufi mystic Rumi, can still my very soul. These artists live at the frontier between the personal and universal, the intimate and the ultimate, the accessible and the unobtainable. This is the same frontier cancer has carried me to and deposited me like a gift. Here, like Mary Oliver, I am "willing to be dazzled — to cast aside the weight of facts and maybe even to float a little above this difficult world." Here I can see with my inner eyes and hear with my inner ears. I can find my own wise way through the world.

Your intuition is your inner compass on your journey with cancer, perhaps your most important navigation tool. It is also essential to retaining your autonomy and not handing your inner authority over to the experts to make crucial decisions for you. Even when I agree to what experts recommend — which is quite often, actually — I wait for my intuition to say yes before I let my mouth say it. In this way, I know I have chosen it 100 percent and won't end up feeling victimized or blaming others for any unwelcome consequences. Whatever happens, I want to know that I acted consciously and responsibly, trusting myself even in my loneliest choices and darkest hours.

3. Creating Your Own Plan

Some cancer patients choose wholly orthodox routes (radiotherapy, surgery and chemotherapy) and others choose wholly alternative routes, avoiding chemical interventions altogether. As I shared earlier in this chapter, I've chosen an integrated route in which I can benefit from both. You will know which is the best way for you to go. I know two women who healed their own cancer (early stage) through diet and natural treatments alone. I know others who have opted for medical interventions and fared equally well. I chose to integrate both approaches, because I saw significant merit in each, and because a terminal diagnosis made me reach for anything credible I could get my hands on.

What made the most sense to me was building my immune system up as much as I could while I underwent other treatments. Immunotherapy, which boosts the body's natural defenses to fight disease, is the big new hope for cancer treatment. It is all about tricking the immune system into attacking the cancer cells. This is a burgeoning industry for Big Pharma, and many oncologists consider immunotherapy the future of cancer care. There are also many natural remedies that can help boost the immune system, which can be so severely compromised by chemotherapy.

I was very drawn to Dr. Dana Flavin, Dr. Muñoz at the San Diego Clinic, and Dr. Contreras at the Oasis of Hope Hospital because they combine natural remedies with synthetic ones, building the immune system up before administering low-dose chemotherapy or proceeding with surgery. These natural treatments include mega doses of Vitamin C and laetrile (also known as B17), hyperthermia (heating the body to fever pitch to shrink the tumors and boost the immune system), and ozone therapy to oxygenate the blood.

You will need to intuit what is right for you, but I urge you to explore your options as fully as you can before committing to a particular path. If you choose a primarily medical route, there are still things you can do to support your body through this experience — like using strengthening supplements, having lymph drainage massages, using detoxing protocols to flush any poisons through your system. What matters most is that it is *your* plan, that you *own it* rather than simply follow along with what you're told to do by your oncologist or nutritionist, that you design its contents and feel at cause in the process instead of at its effect.

Here are some steps that might help you with the process of sorting through the options and making decisions:

1. Create a folder or journal to record all the treatments you are using and want to explore and/or use.

2. Get clear about doses and timings for any drugs or supplements you're already taking. Write down all of this information.

3. Decide how frequently you want to do specific treatments (e.g., massage once a week, detox twice a week, coffee enemas three times a week) and create a weekly schedule on a whiteboard. What you do and how often you do it will depend on your energy levels, your finances and how much time you can commit. The frequencies need to work *for* you, not add to your stress.

4. Create a cancer treatments diary that includes all your medical appointments as

well as your weekly treatments. Factor in recovery times if you are having chemo or radiotherapy. Also, very importantly, mark in time with your family, so they don't lose you to a medical timetable when they most want to be around you and offer their support.

5. Run your treatment plan past your most trusted medical adviser, someone who is open to your choices but will raise red flags if needed.

4. Preserving Your Personhood

I nearly called this book *How to Preserve Your Personhood When You Are Diagnosed with Cancer.* Helping cancer patients preserve their personhood is one of my core purposes for writing it. When my diagnostician said to me, "Don't become a patient, Mrs. Sabbage," I didn't know how transformational and lifesaving that advice would become.

After I was diagnosed, when I found myself sucked into a medical machine that dealt with my disease, not my humanity, that told me when to show up for appointments without asking me if I was available then, and that repeatedly asked me for information already in my file, *personhood* was what I needed the most. Even though the people I was meeting with were, and are, incredibly hardworking, well-intentioned people, some of whom shine with humanity and compassion, they are still part of a system that makes it very hard for them to treat us like sentient beings instead of a medical condition.

I went for an MRI on Good Friday this year, so there were only two nurses on duty to cannulate me (insert a tube in the vein to allow intravenous drug administration) for the injection of the contrast dye they use. Between them, they made seven attempts, and then sent me home because they had failed to access a vein. Both of those nurses had dealt with me before and they always needed to call on someone more experienced to get the cannula in. When I went to that same hospital again for my next CT scan, I saw the following statement written in capital letters on my file: "PATIENT DIFFICULT TO CANNULATE." It made it sound as if the difficulty was about my veins rather than their competence. I go to a clinic once a week for infusions of Vitamin C and they cannulate me the first time almost every time, so the note in my file at the hospital seemed to me like an abdication of responsibility.

Three nurses came to assess my veins, two

attempted the cannulation and failed. Then they called in their supervisor, who came in and made her own attempt. Without even introducing herself or addressing me by my name, she said to me, "You're difficult."

"No," I responded, "I'm Sophie. I understand your nurses have had some trouble with my veins, but that does not make me difficult. Or my veins, for that matter. If you believe I am difficult to cannulate, then I probably will be, but please don't blame me for it."

She was somewhat taken aback, but I needed to speak up for myself. I go to that hospital for scans every three months and I don't want the story that I am "difficult to cannulate" to be perpetuated without justification. My arms are not pincushions. I then helped out the supervisor by telling her which veins were most reliable: the one on the side of my right forearm and several in my hands. Those are more painful, but they're definitely accessible. She cannulated me the first time she tried.

As it turned out, there was some justification. My veins are thin and pop easily even after the needle has gone in. Fellow cancer patients tell me our veins "wise up and run away" when they sense a needle coming, which makes a lot of sense. At the same time, we need to be careful that additional problems are not projected onto our already problematic situations and that we retain our identities as whole human beings with our very own needs and names.

Those kinds of experiences make me determined to preserve my own personhood in any way I can. I trust that this book testifies to my commitment and inspires you to do the same.

Here are some small but significant things I do that make a difference in remaining a person, rather than being only a patient:

1. I let the administrators know when I am available for appointments and asked them to stop sending me letters dictating what times to show up. They call me now instead.

2. I meditate in MRI machines, which are incredibly noisy, because meditating takes me deep inside myself and meditating in an MRI machine gives me a sense of mastering my dominion while reminding me that I don't need quiet to find peace.

3. I say a prayer while the laser strikes my neck and thank God for whatever healing this treatment brings. I don't like the idea of radiation going into my body because it is carcinogenic in itself, so I like to welcome it instead of fighting it in the hope

that my body receives a healing message from my brain.

4. I find out when nurses I trust are on shift and try to book my appointments when they're there.

5. I dress up whenever I go to the hospital. I wear something I feel fabulous in, put on my mascara and lipstick (which I very rarely wear), and show up as if I am going to a dinner party or the theater.

See if you can find your own ways to preserve your personhood when you interact with the medical system. Little things can make a big difference to retaining your dignity and staying *yourself.*

8
DANCING WITH GRIEF

Soon after my diagnosis, it became increasingly difficult for me to move. I became breathless easily and the tumor on my C^3 neck vertebra was excruciatingly painful much of the time. But I knew it was important for me to move my body as much as possible, to take it out into fresh clean air and let nature kiss it. So I went for a walk every day I could, rarely more than twenty minutes out from home and always with my phone in my pocket in case I got into trouble. I wanted to walk alone and feel the pulse of the beauty I live in the midst of — which helped me feel my own.

A few fields away, there is a small herd of horses, usually six or seven, belonging to a neighbor. Their field sometimes needs to be cleared of horse dung, but they are otherwise well kept, and I had walked among them many times since we moved to the countryside. Mostly, they ignored me unless

I approached them, which they permitted in an indifferent kind of way. No doubt eating grass or the hay left out for them was far more interesting than my hand stroking their silky necks. I loved going home with the sweet musty smell of them on my fingers.

Then when I got sick, very sick, something changed. As I entered their field one frosty November morning, I stopped just past the turnstile gate to catch my breath and appreciate their nobility. There were six of them that day, spread out across about an acre of grass, most of them at the other end of the field from where I was standing. The skies were clear blue and I could see two oast houses nestled in a small wood — distinctive circular buildings with conical roofs originally designed for drying hops. We had moved here because this is where my husband was born and his parents are buried. He hadn't been back for several decades, but it felt right to go home with him when Gabriella was born, and I had fallen in love with its distinctive architecture, sea-lined borders, fruit-laden orchards and gentle landscape. All the same, I felt a pang of sadness because we were renting a converted barn and had been planning to buy our forever home before my diagnosis. That seemed entirely impossible now.

That morning, I found I didn't have the energy to walk over to the horses. I stood there yearning to stroke their beautiful faces, when something remarkable happened. A chestnut mare and gray gelding lifted their heads from the grass and started walking toward me. Seconds later the others looked up in unison and followed. Some were at least two hundred yards away so it took a matter of minutes for them all to reach me, but eventually I was fully encircled by horses. The largest, a sixteen-hand gray gelding, nuzzled at my chest while a palomino pony rested its muzzle on my shoulder, and the youngest, still a foal, tentatively smelled the backs of my hands. I was so surprised and delighted, it brought tears to my eyes. I responded by breathing into their noses with my nose to say hello, as they do with each other and as I had seen horse whisperers do. This involved bending down and tilting my head back, which slightly jarred my tumor-obstructed neck, but I didn't care. Something more important was happening, something unexpected and mysterious and sacred that I didn't understand. They stayed with me for nearly forty minutes before I became too tired to continue. I was the one who broke contact before walking home slowly with a lump in my throat and something stirring at the base of my soul.

This experience stayed with me into the evening and unsettled me through the night. Had it really happened? Was it just a one-off random occurrence that wouldn't repeat itself — even though of course I was hoping and praying it would? When I eagerly returned to the field the next morning, I walked through the turnstile gate, stopped about twenty feet in front of it and stood completely still to see what would happen, waiting anxiously. Sure enough, within a few minutes, they lifted their heads from the grass they were chewing and walked purposefully toward me. Another horse circle formed around me. More nuzzles. More neck strokes. More breathing into each other's noses to say hello. But never breaking the circle or dropping their heads to eat the grass again, as horses normally do. They just stood with me, offering me something I could neither explain nor account for except by the strange healing sensation that began pulsing through my veins.

These encounters continued for seven weeks, until I left to fly to Mexico for alternative treatments. I didn't go every day during that period of time, but I went as often as I could and, as long as I was alone, the horses always came. If John or a visiting friend accompanied me, they stayed away. This was between them and me. It was *for* me. Of that I was certain. It was as if they knew I was sick and wanted to warn me, heal me or perhaps simply be with me in my dying days as they might be with each other. This is mostly conjecture, but it felt like I was being treated as one of the herd and this brought me great solace during a time of great fear. It assured me I was part of a greater, grander life force than the one that was dwindling daily in my own body. It diluted the loneliness of no longer being wholly part of this world and alleviated the more terrifying aloneness of beginning to belong to Something Else.

I grew up in the Black Mountains in Wales. Unlike most of my family, who were in love with the Valleys, my spirits were dampened by the gray days and the frequently wet, cloudy and windy climate. Much of the time I didn't want to get up in the mornings and I became easily depressed. Our home, an old mill converted lovingly by my dad when my siblings and I were small children, was down in a valley, and the surrounding mountains seemed to close in on me like thick walls. I longed to escape.

And I did. On the back of a horse. Across the ridges and above the clouds. Sometimes with friends, sometimes alone, often for hours at a time. The heaviness would lift from my chest, and my eyes would open to the soft rolling wonder all around me. That was when I understood why my family was so betrothed to this place. The Valleys seemed to breathe like sentient beings infused with the memories of millennia. Leaning forward and galloping into the wind was the best way I knew how to silence the incessant inner commentary of self-criticism that marked my teenage years. Perhaps this is where my deep affinity with horses is rooted. I guess they were healing me even then.

Abraham Maslow describes a peak experience as "the awareness of an 'ultimate truth' . . . that arrives, almost instantly, in an experience that fills you with wonder, ecstasy and awe." I had one of these experiences on horseback in my mid-thirties when I went on a riding safari to the Okavango Delta in Botswana, a vast inland oasis in the central part of the Kalahari Desert. The delta forms over the course of a month when the Okavango River drains the summer rainfall. It triples in size when the flood peaks in the winter months and briefly hosts one of the most intense concentrations of wildlife on earth.

You need to be an experienced rider to do this safari, adept enough to act fast and stay seated if a hippo surfaces from the water as you canter through it. Being on a horse allows you to get very near to the animals, as you follow game paths used only by herds of wildebeest or families of elephants as they move across the golden floodplains. Mounted high above the reeds, you turn a corner and they are right there, unfazed by the arrival of other animals and seemingly unaware of the humans on their backs. It is as breathtakingly close to nature as you can get.

Toward the end of my time there, we galloped around the bend in a river one morning and I found myself side by side with several giraffes, moving at equal pace but with much larger strides. For several minutes I was in among them. Just. Like. That. I was at once immensely powerful and equally helpless, inside space and outside time, the water splashing my ankles, the wind singing through the grass, the unity of all things deluging my being while I was running, running, running with giraffes.

We rode back to camp that afternoon in silence. There were no words to express it. They fail me still, like fading memories of faint footsteps on a disappearing road.

That same night, I dreamt my beloved friend and teacher Brad was dying. The last time I had seen him, only a few weeks before, he had been holding on to his last threads of lucidity as Lewy body dementia clamped his brilliant, beautiful mind in its iron vise of delusion and forgetfulness, and Parkinson's rolled through his body like an unstoppable landslide. Later his wife told me he had reserved those threads for me, that my final visit to his home in California had seemed to reach inside his last cache of creativity, clarity and contribution to the world. For three whole days he had remembered who he was and what he was here to give.

There were no phone signals in the delta, but as we rode out that day and stood silently on a hill, observing a herd of wildebeest, I felt his spirit pass as surely as the thunder of hooves and splashing water when I ran, ran, ran with giraffes. I turned to my traveling companion, who also knew and loved him, and told her Brad was gone. She took it as fact and once again we returned to the camp in awestruck, tear-stained silence.

The next day we were driven back to a town with Wi-Fi connection, where I made a phone call that confirmed Brad's passing. And so began a grief that would draw out like the Kalahari Desert until cancer taught me to channel it like summer rainfall into a vibrant delta teeming with kaleidoscopic life.

It was on my fourth visit to my field of horses that these memories cascaded in on a wave of gratitude for such treasured experiences — as well as sadness that they were so completely and finally behind me. As the horses stood around me like the standing stones of Stonehenge, I realized I would never ride again. My spine could not tolerate any jarring. My stay on earth seemed so very limited now. Time had frozen. It was neither *chronos* (chronological and sequential) nor *kairos* (expansive and indeterminate). Instead, it shriveled into a tight ball of terrified confusion and disbelief, passively waiting for something to happen. That something arrived in a wet field on a cold winter day as I bent down into my memories, the ones I had and the ones I would never have, and my heart broke, like a dam, with grief.

THE NATURE OF GRIEF

This experience was revelatory for me and profoundly healing. It was the beginning of a journey into grief I hadn't made before, even through all my years of involvement in therapeutic practices and personal development. Of all the human emotions, grief was the one I passed by like a stranger on the pavement or reserved only for momentous, earth-cracking losses. Brad had built my emotional intelligence in so many ways during the years I had known him. He had taught me how to pass through fear instead of suppressing or controlling it, how to release anger in ways that harm no one, how to drop resentment like a hot stone without condoning what I object to, and how to truly love another human being, including the one I have woken up and gone to sleep with every day since I was born. He called it "love-ability": the ability to love and be loved. But I never saw him grieve and he hadn't taught me about the nature of grief. This was, perhaps, his emotional blind spot and, as one of his heirs, mine.

I understood grief to be an emotional response to loss. I had certainly felt it at times of significant loss, such as the death of a loved one or the end of a cherished relationship. I also knew it was a healthy and healing response to loss, both psychologically and spiritually, in spite of the predominantly negative light in which it is perceived in our culture. It is seen as something unpleasant and uncomfortable to get through. Often we attempt to manage it by retreating from the world in order to get over a great sorrow before reconnecting, all bright and chirpy again. But this is not grief. It is fear of grief and the avoidance of grief. It is a profound misunderstanding of grief's essence and purpose.

Essentially, there are two types of emotion: those that *separate* us from ourselves, others and life (fear, anger, envy, bitterness, resentment, depression, despair) and those that *connect* us to ourselves, others and life (joy, peace, love, awe, serenity, sadness, grief). Grief connects. When we grieve well, it opens rather than closes the heart. This is why it heals. Grief picks you up from the depths of your despair and frees you to move forward again. This much I had learned, but no more.

Before I got cancer, I had bought the myth that grief can help you find "closure." It doesn't. It passes through our lives like a river through mountains or the flow of blood through veins. It is emotional oxygen, as vital to our health and well-being as the air we breathe and the water we drink. It is our best, most appropriate response to regret, loss, bereavement, hurt, privation, disappointment and change. It is the transitional bridge from the life we wanted or expected to live to the life we are actually living, the one riddled with out-of-the-blue setbacks and letdowns. Like being diagnosed with terminal cancer when you're the adoring mother of a dazzling four-year-old daughter and married to the kindness in mankind.

Grief is a hugely neglected part of the cancer experience, usually held in numb abeyance until the end is nigh. Yet I have come to recognize it as one of the great healing forces in my life, and my inadequate attention to it previously as likely one of the primary reasons for my disease. At some point in those early post-diagnosis days, when tracing the emotional roots of my cancer, I discovered that Chinese medicine associates the lungs with two things: inspiration and *grief.* Anger resides in the liver, fear in the kidneys, and grief in the lungs. Given that I have lung cancer and grief was the emotion I had most neglected in my life, this made perfect sense. It also begged the question, "What have I not been grieving and why?"

Answering that question began with looking at my losses — not just the big deaths and endings, which still loitered like ghosts in my attic — but the less obvious hurts, regrets, and disappointments that lay strewn across the carpet of my life. The name-calling on the playground — *by* me as well as *to* me. The edge of the dance floor I looked on from as a teenager. The men I loved but was invisible to. The jobs I wanted but didn't get. The babies I longed for but didn't have. The flat-stomached, pert-breasted bodies I envied — and seemed to see everywhere — because they weren't mine. The lonely years that stretched across my outwardly successful thirties when my business was brimming, my confidence was growing, my personal relationships were failing, and my thirsty heart was drying up like an empty well. The distance, now closed, between my siblings and me. The books I never wrote. The poems I never published. The talks I never gave. The failures I never admitted to. The hurts I inflicted on others. The friendships I neglected and the friends who neglected me. The thousand bushels I hid my light under. The deep-down sensitivity I believed made me incompatible with this world.

This process was epic for me. My terror was immeasurable in those early weeks, but my grief outran it by miles. Looking back, I realize how grief kept me connected to the natural order at a time when terror could have torn me from the truth of things like a riptide.

My terminal diagnosis has meant that, while mourning the catalogue of regrets and losses that permeate my past, I also grieve what is not yet lost. The dreams I haven't given voice to. The ripening of my little girl into womanhood. The wrinkled withering of my husband into beneficent old age. The quiet timely surrendering of my heart's desire to offer myself up to the world and ensure my life counted for something more than personal happiness or success. The deepening lines that carve my life like a map on my face. My well-earned retreat into gentler winds in the winter of days with my beloved John, while Gabriella rises into her purpose like a blood-red sun on a black-and-silver sea.

There is no limit to this grief and no closure. Instead, there is grieving the end of life while keeping life alive. With cancer, there is what you might lose if you don't make it, but also what you will lose if you do. There are a great number of losses that come even if you survive: your hair when you undergo chemotherapy or brain radiation; your ability to work and earn money (a huge loss for me when I was forced to close the business I had been building for twenty years); friends who fall away because the cussed selfishness of the human condition overthrows compassion or because mortality is just too hard for them to face; vitality, energy and resilience you once took for granted; favorite food and drink you have chosen not to eat anymore (champagne, roast lamb and Marmite, to name a few I crave sometimes); your perceived loss of pride or dignity because you need to rely on others when you have so long resisted doing so; your ability to feel, as the Arabian proverb says, "the wind of heaven, which blows between a horse's ears."

Grief is essential to healing because it doesn't hold on to things. It lets them go. It is the only part of us that knows how to let go. That's what it began to do for me in the field that day, encircled by horses I felt sure could contain the flood. Grief releases and redeems me layer upon battered layer. It keeps on giving. Unbidden, unexpected and unbound. My cancer needed me to grieve and I needed cancer to discover my grief.

I grow downward because of it. I have stronger roots. You see, we grieve that which we have loved and do love, so when you feel grief, you feel love. And there is nothing more healing than love. Grief keeps love alive, like raising Lazarus from the dead cells of your darkest memories and deepest longings, then dancing with him into the morning. I believe that is what it is doing for me. Raising me from the dead. Perhaps literally. Because living is fueled by loving. And love needs grief in order to fulfill itself.

THREE GATEWAYS TO GRIEF

You don't need to have lung cancer, in particular, to awaken your grief and let it heal your life. Any cancer will cut this vein because any cancer will confront you with your mortality and the possibility of losing all you hold dear. In the first edition of this book, I omitted this chapter because I couldn't see how to do grief justice or walk my readers into a country I have only just learned to navigate.

While I was discovering the nature of grief, I created a workshop on this theme. It takes people deep into their hitherto invisible sorrows with skillful facilitation and support. I hope to continue offering this in different formats in the future, but this book will likely reach many more readers than can attend my courses. If it reaches you, and you recognize the healing potential of grief on your cancer journey, or simply in your life, I recommend engaging some kind of professional grief practitioner to support you in this endeavor. It will likely be challenging and, at times, too painful to engage with alone. I have had moments of being so bent by grief I thought I would never stand straight again. At the very least, invite a trusted friend or partner to walk this road with you.

While I can't give you the full grief course experience here, I have created some simple, powerful ways to unlock your sorrow and bring it into the light of day. This alone will be great medicine. So here are three gateways to grief:

1. List Your Losses

This is a free-flow written exercise in a journal in which you list every loss, disappointment and regret you can think of when you review your life. It does not need to be in any order. When it comes to mind, write it down. No editing! It doesn't matter how big or small it seems. If it comes into your consciousness, it needs attention. Your body is riddled with disappointments and regrets.

We carry them in our cells, ignoring them as meaningless, discounting them as "no big deal" or numbing them out with foods, drugs, sex and alcohol.

As you write this list, breathe as consciously as you can and notice what you feel in your body. You may feel a lump in your throat, tightness in your chest or churning in your stomach. Let these feelings expand. Give them permission. You may not have to do all this. You may just start weeping as your write. If so, go ahead and cry your precious heart out. Remember, snot is good. Snot is expelled pain!

2. Lay Down Your Regrets

Review your list and pick out any significant regrets. Make a new list of these regrets so you can give them special attention. I cut a very deep vein of regret in my life, so my list was shockingly long and its impact devastating. For example:

- I was lacerated by regret for the self-destructive actions of my teens and twenties, which I recognized as my part in getting cancer in my forties. I wanted to take full responsibility for this without blaming myself or discounting the other contributory factors.
- I deeply regretted losing touch with a close

friend from university, named Suzy. I looked her up on social media to no avail and felt heartbroken at the prospect of dying without telling her how much she meant to me.

- I was heartbroken about never writing a book, which is what I had wanted to do since I was ten years old but kept putting off year after year. I loved the vocation I had chosen but couldn't forgive myself for setting this other ambition aside. It felt like an open wound in my soul.

- I was haunted by the suicide of one of my closest friends, whose longing for God outran his willingness to stay on earth and whose regret about his decision was carried across the river Thames, into which he had jumped from a South London bridge, by screams of "Help!" when he hit the water. I had noticed his state of mind at our last encounter but hadn't called or listened or intervened.

In each case, when I was bent double with the pain of raw remorse, these words kept streaming from my lips: "I wish I had . . . I wish I hadn't . . . If only I had . . . if only I hadn't . . . if only . . . if only . . . if only . . ." My head would shake from side to side with every "I wish" and "if only," each one peeling back another layer of regret from the one before. Afterward, in the calm after the storm, I was able to make clear choices in response to my regrets. This was one of the most liberating things I've ever done.

So, once you have identified your regrets, choose one at a time to work with and follow the steps of this process:

The Regret Process

1. Close your eyes and focus on the regret you have chosen.
2. Say out loud, "I wish I had/hadn't . . . if only I had/hadn't . . ." and express whatever follows.
3. Shake your head from side to side to connect with your emotions.
4. Feel your feelings fully.
5. Let go of your regret and choose what to do.

And just in case you're wondering . . . I forgave myself (fully and finally). I wrote a book, which you are now reading, and when the *Observer* wrote an article about it, my university friend found me.

3. Honor Your Hopes

The extent to which you engage with this will depend on the seriousness of your diagnosis and prognosis. If you have stage four cancer and your oncologist has been reckless enough to put a timeframe on your remaining lifespan, this step is a must. But frankly, it's a must whatever stage your cancer has reached or, indeed, your life has reached. You may not even have cancer. You may be cruising through life on the assumption you will make it to a ripe old age and manage to resurrect all your dashed dreams before you reach the finish line. If that is the case, WAKE UP! Your future is not inevitable. It is not a given. It can be snatched away in a second when you are least expecting it. So I invite you to look down the lens of your half-baked hopes and unadorned dreams to see what grief, healing, and resurrection have to offer you. Here's how:

1. Write down at least ten hopes and/or dreams you have set aside or given up on, but still hold in your heart (however secretly).

2. Truthfully and bravely choose which ones to let go of (once and for all) and which ones to resurrect (once and for all).

3. For each one you choose to let go of, find a way to say good-bye. Write a poem, paint a picture or find something that symbolizes your dream. Then bury it in the ground, send it out to sea or set it aflame. You decide. It just needs to be

wholehearted and deliberate. You can also create a collective good-bye, like a collage, if it is too much to do it one by one. As you do this, feel your sorrow.

4. For each one you choose to resurrect, write down a clear plan about how you are going to bring it back to life. You could use The Purpose Process in Chapter Four to achieve this.

For me, one consequence of picking up some dreams I had swept under the rug has been a newfound willingness to shine my light in corners of the world I believed were meant for those more beautiful or brilliant than me. For example, I started to write, which I have wanted to do for decades. It began with my blog, originally titled *My Journey of Wellness with Terminal Illness* — which led to this book just nine months later. I now see that I didn't simply neglect my intention to write. This was its time. I never wanted to write fiction, because I have never had that great an imagination or been a natural storyteller. I still struggle to make up stories for Gabriella when she asks me to. Even at school, I was top of the class in English most of the time but rubbish at thinking of original things to write about. Once I borrowed the idea for a story from my best friend, Lydia, who was a wonderful writer. It was about an otter and I got an A. But I felt embarassed more than pleased about this because it seemed so fraudulent, even though the actual writing was mine.

I prefer writing about real life and all that Life with a capital L reveals to us about who we are, where we've come from and what we're capable of becoming. Cancer gave me a landscape to write about that is relevant and meaningful to anyone who has arrived on the cliff edge of their life, a place where they can see the horizon of their years and the commotion of their memories in the harbor. I can now call myself an author because living with cancer provided fresh soil in which I could sow my seeds of service, for which I am deeply grateful.

LET THE RIVER FLOW

Living with a terminal illness keeps the channels of grief open. While it continues to strip me of the deepest underlying *dis-eases* I have carried through my life, there is no ducking the possibility of dying before I turn silver and no plugging the underground river that flows through my days. It rises and falls like a tide, sometimes crashing with the force of a tsunami, sometimes lapping quietly on my shore. It responds to changes in the weather, lifeshocks that ensue from scans, treatments, side effects and symptoms, or from being embedded in various cancer communities where we are all too frequently confronted with our mortality.

During my last stay at a clinic in Mexico, two patients died, and another just a month after I had left. One was a young Korean man whose father has now taken his place in history's caravan of parched sorrows for lost children. The other was a woman from Kazakhstan who fought for life with her frail, skeletal frame, her body as devastated by chemo, radiation and surgery as it was by cancer. She leaves behind three children, the youngest of whom is just five — the same age as Gabriella as I write.

The woman who died shortly after returning home was an American, about my age, with stage four esophageal cancer, and was finding it impossible to eat. When I last saw her she was slowly starving to death. She lay on the bed next to me one morning, receiving ozone therapy, crushed by despair at the prospect of leaving her three teenage children and resigned to this inevitability. I had no solace for her. I could but join her in her inconsolable pain.

For all my newfound insight into the healing power of grief, the prospect of leaving my darling Gabriella, who begs me not to go away for treatments and misses me terribly when I do, remains more than I can bear. We're as close as sea and sand. I have nothing enlightened or brave to say about it. I cannot accept it. I will not accept it. I do not accept it. Sometimes I wonder if God gave her to me so late in my life because He knew I would need a reason bigger than my fear of dying to make me bend over backward to stay.

One of the forces that helps me bend over backward is *hope.* Buffeted by cautious oncologists and political cowards who limit treatment options for "terminal" patients in the name of refusing to peddle "false hope," I have ridden it like a horse across the valleys. Just as there is no such thing as grief that brings "closure," there is no such thing as "false hope." There is hope or there is none. Hope is a projection into a desired future, a feeling that something wanted or longed for could perhaps become reality. Hope doesn't make promises. It just hopes. And it is one of the most potent motivating forces I know.

There is no ducking the "terminal" nature of my illness. I am reminded of it constantly. It is not a diagnosis you forget. But too much has happened since then for me to live into that inevitability. Nothing is cast in stone. I was never going to ride a horse again, but have. I was never going to teach a workshop again, but have. I was never going to write a book, but have. I am done with predictions and inevitabilities. Instead, I choose to live on the sacred frontier of *Not Knowing,* where the world as I imagine it meets the world as it actually is. This is where I stand still, poised for epiphany, ready to break for freedom from whatever I believed was so but wasn't. *Not Knowing* takes me in when I have no place else to go.

The horses don't come to me anymore. Since my cancer receded into a fraction of itself and my essential wellness returned, they carry on grazing when I arrive in their field, not even lifting their heads to acknowledge my presence. They still let me breathe into their noses when I walk over to them, as if some memory of our encounters lingers among the herd, but I am really just another human passing through. I find this deeply comforting. When I am anxious that my cancer might be on the rise again, or freaking out during PST (pre-scan tension), I visit the field to see how they respond to me. If they ignore me, I reckon I'm okay. I consider them my equine scanners. Sensing disease like cancer detection dogs. Alerting me to signs of danger. And, unlike CT scanners, radiation-free.

I can't confirm this, of course. I'm just going by my own experience with these beautiful horses, which stands out like a beacon on my journey and confirms my faith in Something Else on this side of the crossing. This is who I am. Wide-eyed with wonder. Unwrapping life's mysteries. Letting cancer free my spirit *before* it leaves my body. Dancing with grief.

You see, once you have invited grief into your life, you must let it stay. Remember, it is love's beloved. They are eternally betrothed. This isn't to say you should go about your days in perpetual mourning, weighed down by the burden of accumulated sorrow. Quite the opposite. As I have come to understand it, sorrow is just one of grief's outlets and grief is not the emissary of misery but a gateway back to joy. I became uncharacteristically perky in its wake, as if it had imbued me with a homeopathic dose of joie de vivre. My friends expressed concern. Who was this perky person with positivity oozing out of her pores like refined honey and finding implausible joy in what seemed flawlessly catastrophic and cruel? This was not the intense, deep-diving, glass-is-half-empty Sophie they

229

had known before I got cancer. They didn't know what had gotten into me. They didn't know I had been infused with tributaries of grief that stream from origins older than my ancestors and merge into a river that carries no anger or remorse or pain.

9
BREAKING THE SHELL

I have been very struck by the difference between patients I meet in my oncology center in a local hospital, which offers orthodox center treatments, and those I meet in alternative clinics I attend.

In the oncology center, there is a pervasive despondency and numbed-out silence as patients wait for treatment and reserve their conversations for their companions. You can feel cancer suckling on people's terror and parading around the hospital like a triumphant conqueror, scalps in its hands. The patients I have connected with in the oncology center seem to be going along with what their oncologists have told them, without question or inquiry, treating their disease as a terrible misfortune to be endured and survived as stoically as possible. This is partly down to a combination of the British stiff-upper-lip culture and the gray sheen of jaded service in our overstretched hospitals.

It is quite possible that sitting in some of the chemo chairs are some of the most heuristic and innovative patients alive, people who, like me, are withholding from this audience their off-piste treatment adventures while in an environment more likely to judge than support them.

Nonetheless, the disconsolate *why is this happening to me?* atmosphere permeates the oncological environment like winter fog in a deep Snowdonia valley. I have learned to fill my pockets with protective crystals so it doesn't permeate my body too.

In contrast, while in alternative clinics, I often meet patients who are wide-eyed and curious about their cancer, wondering what it has to teach them and why it has visited them at this time, in this form, in this way. Even if they have no answers, they feel certain that cancer carries a message, revelation or gift for them, which they are determined to receive and learn from — if only they can figure out how. They see cancer as a blessing and respond to it with a firm faith in some higher purpose at work in their lives.

Sometimes this faith can seem naïve, even blind, and smells of disowned terror coated in false positivity and hollow prayer. Other times it resonates like a double bass in a perfectly tuned orchestra, undeniable in its purpose and certain of its place. There is a lightness of being in these patients, a strength of spirit, an acceptance of the disease, a surprising joy in its presence — and a narrative of humor, healing and hope.

At one of these clinics, I met a Colombian woman with late-stage ovarian cancer that had spread to her colon. She concealed her bald head with a beautiful, customized brunette wig, which she loved because it was always shiny and never needed to be washed. She had been wearing a permanent colon bag ever since her colostomy. When I asked her how it felt to live with that, she smiled quizzically, as if my question was strange, and replied, "It is nothing. I am alive!"

I had lunch with another woman in the same clinic who had recently been diagnosed with liver cancer that had metastasized to her lungs. When I said, "Bless your heart," in response to her story (something I have since stopped saying because it is woefully inadequate and patronizing), she laughed and said, "No, bless my liver, please."

These people are in a bigger conversation with their illness than merely the desire to get rid of and overcome it. That's not what they want — or not all they want. They are not exempt from the fear and sorrow that bathe in cancer's backwash, but they have turned into it like children who have stripped down to their underwear in winter rain and run into the ice-cold waves on an unexpected shoreline, squealing when they first feel the water but unable to resist its appeal. There is something here to be discovered, something more than the freezing water that peppers them with goose bumps and makes their teeth chatter like maracas. We are engaged with a mystery, which seems to rise like a mist from the surface of our suffering and beg us to know it and be known.

Both these groups of patients ask the same essential question, but for diametrically opposed reasons: "Why me?" In most cases the subtext of that question is either "This shouldn't be happening, I haven't done anything to deserve it" or "What did I do to deserve this? What have I done wrong?" Either way, this is a victimized "done to" position, inviting the mind to judge, interpret, and draw false, negative conclusions that send you spiraling into further victimization and remorse. They remind me of a minister from New England I met at one cancer clinic. He had been diagnosed with colon cancer but took it upon himself to corner his fellow patients in their infusion chairs with a Bible and crucifix, trying to convince them that Satan needed to be cast out of their bodies in order for them to heal.

I think I was the only one he couldn't pin down that week. He tried several times, but I held firm boundaries by saying no whenever he approached me to "discuss your relationship with God." I found him deeply presumptuous, not to mention hypocritical and arrogant. It was like having personified mindtalk sitting down next to me at dinner and forcing itself upon me in the name of saving me from my sins. Eventually, I put a stop to his pestering by telling him bluntly, "I need you to get this, then leave me alone. God and me . . . we're good."

I want to be loud and clear about this in case you're heading off down a guilty, shameful, self-recriminating tunnel, because there's absolutely no cheese at the end of it: *Cancer is not a punishment. Cancer is not proof of how worthless you are. Cancer does not confirm that you are a failure as a human being.*

That said, there is a way to ask "Why me?" from a position of responsibility and inquiry. This has two subtexts. First, in my experience, there is one primary question to ask in any challenging situation, the answer to which can deliver personal transformation: "What is my part (in the problem and the solution)?" For me, this was about fully owning my part in having cancer, from eating disorders and smoking when I was younger to neglecting my grief for so many years — and also unconsciously taking on other people's negative feelings such that I felt them in my own body as if they were mine. It was only in my thirties that Brad gave me a name for this — "body empath" — and I began to learn how to manage what I have since come to recognize as a blessing and a curse. Indeed, I took the question, "What's my part?" so seriously I created a chart called "The Roots of My Cancer" so I could take total responsibility for as much as possible, including environmental factors — without blaming myself unfairly. There were factors at play other than my behavior. For example, my oncologist told me I had a faulty gene, which he saw as the primary cause, but I reckon that would have given me a one-in-six chance of getting lung cancer. My own choices likely made that one in three.

The second subtext to "Why me?" is this: Why is this event happening to this human being at this time in this context? What is the universe trying to tell me? What is the event calling me out to be and to do? Since meeting one of the greatest influences of my life, Dr. Brad Brown, when I was twenty-five years old, I have come to trust that the events of my life are not just random coincidental occurrences — my interpretations of which determine the quality of my experience — but opportunities for my awakening and transformation. I loved him like a father and miss him daily since his death in 2007. I have often longed for his counsel and reassurance on this arduous pilgrimage, but I have been profoundly sustained by the central tenet of his teaching: *"There is no event by which and through which Life itself is not trying to awaken you to your highest and noblest self."*

Imagine that! There is *no event* that is not inviting you to become your best self — even the self you are destined to be. Most of us have had traumatic and painful experiences, but how many of us have looked back on them and said, "I'm so glad I had that experience. I didn't know it at the time, but it was one of the best things that could have happened to me. It made me who I am"? Dr. Brown extended this notion by proposing that we don't need to wait until we're looking back on these events to claim the gifts they have to offer. We can engage with them in the present tense and proactively pluck the pearl from the oyster shell, even in the face of great suffering.

Brown lived with Parkinson's disease for some years before he died, and I witnessed him claim the disease's gifts faster than it stole his faculties. When he was first diagnosed, his doctor told him, "Parkinson's dooms you to live consciously." In other words, he needed to tell his arm to tell his hand to tell his fingers to move his pen across the page. His handwriting got smaller and smaller with each attempt to write until he could barely read what he had written. Eventually, he couldn't write at all. It was like watching a computer crash. Everything shut down.

He froze more often than he got the shakes. I recall being with him once when he was laid out for three hours on his living room floor at his home in California, unable to move or speak. At first, I was so scared I stood there like a statue, as frozen and dumbfounded as he was, not knowing what to do for this man who had served me as no other and whom I loved so very much. I wasn't ready to lose him or grow up without him, and I couldn't bear to see his helplessness, but I managed to sit on the floor next to him and sandwich his hand in mine to assure him he was not alone. As I did so, I noticed a light blazing at the backs of his eyes and serenity stroking his face. Nothing moved but his belly, which rippled with laughter and disarmed my terror while a few quiet tears simultaneously rolled down his cheeks.

Later, when his muscles began to move again and he was able to sit up and sip some water, I asked him why he had been laughing.

"What would Life give someone who has dedicated his whole life to living consciously?" he replied. "A disease that 'dooms' me to do just that!"

This was how he slipped so graciously down his steep mountain to the inevitable ocean below, opening to the gifts of his disease and letting every painful and limiting event awaken him to his highest and noblest self.

Since my own diagnosis, I've often thought about how Brad met his disease, Parkinson's, as well as the Lewy body dementia that accompanied it and dragged him into an underworld where his wife was a stranger and his home a foreign land. It forced him to fight for what had once come so easily to him. The dementia dangled truth like lush fruit near his dry lips — and then yanked it away before he could taste it. It sent him back to the kindergarten of awakening to learn *a, b, c* again. In one of his lucid moments, near the end, after I had expressed my desire to take his pain away and inquired as to how he could bear another day of it, he held my shaking hand in his firm grasp and assured me, "The light is always there, my friend. The light is *always* there."

"What would Life give you to wake you up to who you are and what's really possible?" That was the question Brown asked the thousands of people he trained and coached over several decades. And he always wrote "Life" with a capital L, as if it were another word for God. This wasn't about what life would give you if you had done something bad. Quite the opposite. It was about what life would give you if you were asleep to some part of yourself that needed to be witnessed, enlivened and honored.

So what would Life give a woman who devoted her life to serving others but hadn't learned to truly serve herself? What would Life give a visionary leader who had lost her vision and a writer who had never allowed herself to write? What would Life give someone who knows how to confront the mind, dissolve fear and heal the spirit but hasn't found a big enough context in which to channel those skills toward making the difference she is capable of making? What would Life give someone who still had not found peace with the body she had battled since childhood, despite years of therapeutic effort to that end? Stage four lung cancer. That's what. Just as the cancer pandemic tilts toward 1 in 2.5 people being diagnosed, while its psychological roots and emotional impact remain largely unattended and its true nature remains unknown. It was my perfect storm.

That was how Brad taught me to relate to the events of my life, not only as the triggers of my unconscious mind but as encounters with truth — lifeshocks knocking on my door over and over until I open my eyes to *Sophie as She Really Is* and *Things as They Really Are.* I think this is what the thirteenth-century poet Rumi meant when he said, "The sea water begs the pearl to break its shell." We are shepherded out of self-deception and darkness through the unbidden, unexpected and often unwanted events of our lives — including cancer. This is life's compass showing us the way.

So how do we listen to these events and pluck the pearl from the oyster shell? If you sense that cancer has something to teach you and that you have been given cancer for a purpose, how do you discover what that purpose is? It can't be figured out or merely interpreted. It is revealed through your experience and discerned through your innate wisdom.

I remember my parents being very alarmed when I told them I was going to a clinic in Mexico instead of having my brain radiated in the UK. My dad did a couple of hours of research online to find out more about it. He has been super-supportive from the start of all this and wanted to be helpful in any way he could, but when he told me he'd read an article saying the doctor who ran this clinic was a "quack," I barked at him.

"Of course you found an article like that. All pioneering oncologists are criticized for being quacks, because they're offering alternatives to Big Pharma drugs and that is a threat to the trillion-dollar cancer industry. I have done weeks of research compared to your couple of hours, so can you please trust me on this instead of assuming you know better?"

I regretted being so prickly and realized afterward that I was navigating my way through extremely unfamiliar water while my life was on the line — and I wasn't yet trusting myself. So . . . what would Life give me to wake me up to that mistrust? My dad, whose opinion can raise or rock my confidence more than most, questioning my judgment. I came to see that nothing less than roo percent faith in my own wisdom would cut it at this time. There was a little room for error, but no room for misgivings or self-doubt.

I was choosing to steer my own ship through the storm instead of handing my treatment over to medical professionals. I was taking a big risk by putting my own wisdom at the wheel and using my own ingenuity as the rudder. It was time to trust myself as I never had before. I didn't need to convince other people I was doing the right thing, I only needed to convince myself. From that point on, I took full responsibility for my treatment plan and my choices, and I haven't looked back. That experience gifted me with the long-sought trust in myself that now infuses my cells and colors almost all my days.

I remember how in those first few months after my diagnosis, my brain throbbed from the tumors. I became very sensitive to noise and couldn't tolerate anger — whether my own or other people's. Stress, irritation, resentment and self-pity suddenly seemed as life threatening as alcohol and sugar. It was as if I could feel my tumors spring to life in their presence and rub their hands in glee. "Mmm. Yummy. Breakfast." It was that palpable. So I learned to operate at a different frequency, to let my anger go more quickly (something I had always found hard to do), and to live in an almost perpetual state of forgiveness. This state brought with it a deep and abiding peace, the like of which I'd never known. This was the pearl I plucked from the oyster shell. It took cancer in my brain to teach me how to forgive in seconds and how to melt anger at will.

There were so many events like those, awakening my spirit and gracing my existence, even when my fear was at its height. As an example, here is an excerpt from my blog at that time:

There is a profound irony to living with advanced cancer. It was supposed to take me down, but instead it has raised me up . . . The tornado of utmost urgency I was swept up in by my terminal diagnosis has been stilled by the extreme patience needed to stay the course with challenging and painful treatments while waiting, hoping, praying for some sign of progress. It's like meditating with a gun to my head.

Most surprising of all is experiencing such wellness in response to grave illness. I am tired, yes, and have limitations that are hard to adjust to sometimes, but there is a vitality coming into my body that I haven't known before. Part of it comes from healthy eating, disciplined detoxing, a tumor-inhibiting drug I am taking and drinking truly wretch-worthy Chinese herbs three times a day. And part comes from a light that can only be found in the heart of darkness. When everything is blacker than black, there it is: The light of the spirit? Of faith? Of bending into Reality and glimpsing God dancing down the street for joy? I don't know. I feel it in my cells as surely as I feel my disease and I trust it will sustain me through whatever dark days lie ahead. Because I am as riddled with miracles as I am with tumors. Somehow, those two are bedfellows, not adversaries — part of the same deal.

Recently, I heard Dr. Contreras speaking about cancer at his hospital in Mexico. He's an oncologist by profession who has dedicated his life to ending cancer, one patient at a time. I was expecting him to focus on the disease, its causes and the treatments he has developed (which he did on other occasions when he spoke). Instead, he spoke of cancer as a gift. "Justice," he suggests, is getting what you deserve — appropriate punishment. "Mercy" is not getting what you deserve — unqualified clemency. But "grace" is getting what you don't deserve and letting it transform your life. I know what he means. I am battered by blessings. And if feeling strangely, unexpectedly grateful for this mortifying disease is what he was talking about, then little by little, inch by inch, I find myself living in a state of grace.

Cancer, like any life-threatening experience, is more than a disease to survive or succumb to. It is an opportunity to change, to become more of yourself, not less, and to transform your perceptions, even if you can't change the course of your disease. I can, for example, offer you this book and I can share what I am up to in the hope that this will inspire you to make your own wise choices. We can do everything in our power to stay alive in the face of an illness that has outmaneuvered our best scientists for decades, but none of us is ultimately in control of the outcome. There is a divine lottery at work that we have no say in and no real power to change.

Just recently a woman who is part of a cancer community I belong to lost her husband. She did everything she could for him, but is now left to her grief with two small children. We are losing people, many people, every day. I can't know why I am still here when he isn't and I won't burden myself with the perceived unfairness of it all. But I can be grateful for the days I've been given and sobered by these continual reminders of how many people don't make it. They all glisten like a blanket of stars just before dawn draws back the darkness, awakening us to the exuberant bestowal of another day and our willingness to make of it a memory worth keeping and joy worth claiming. This is the true power we have on this journey. It is the one thing we can hold on to and continue to control.

This is what I mean by "cancer whispering" — tuning in to the language of our illness and translating its messages. Sometimes it is telling us something we need to correct in the way we are living our lives, something that could support our healing and recovery. Sometimes it is telling us something about ourselves that we have forgotten or discounted, a quality to fall back on like a bed of feathers or truth to reignite like a naked flame. And sometimes it is telling us something about the nature of reality that allows us to nestle in the folds of the universe and let go.

If cancer whispering is an ability you want

to develop as you steer your ship through these unchartered waters, then instead of "Why me?" and "What did I do wrong?" these are the kinds of questions you can ask:

- What behaviors does my cancer call on me to change?
- What beliefs and judgments does my cancer invite me to challenge?
- What emotions does my cancer invite me to release or express?
- What have I shut down or ignored that I can no longer ignore?
- What ways of being is my cancer exposing that I didn't want to look at before it came along?
- Where in my life is my cancer calling me to be more authentic?
- Where in my life is my cancer calling me to be more vulnerable and human?
- Where in my life is my cancer calling me to be more forgiving and loving?
- What is my cancer reminding me to value that I have forgotten or neglected?
- What unexpected gifts have come my way since I was diagnosed?
- What is my cancer teaching me about my relationship with myself?
- What is my cancer teaching me about my relationship with others?
- What is my cancer teaching me about my

relationship with life itself?

You can also ask most of these questions in relation to any specific lifeshock you have on your journey. Just substitute "my cancer" for "this lifeshock" and see what answers you get. I suggest you do this about your cancer first, because that will help you enter into this discovery process while you are still learning to notice and engage with specific lifeshocks. It will deliver riches in and of itself. However, once you have done this and become more confident with homing in on specific events in your journey, you will start finding pearls in the most unexpected oysters, grace in the most unwanted encounters and peace at the bottom of your pain.

To stir your own wisdom and give you a picture of what this exploration can look like, here are some of my own answers to the above questions (in a form you might also want to try for yourself — a letter to my disease):

Dear Cancer,

I was so scared of you when I first met you and so angry that you had invaded my tidy life. I was finally happy. Living with the deeply loving husband I had held out for until I was forty and the turbocharged daughter I had been told it was too late for me to have. I thought you were going to take everything away — my mobility, creativity and lucidity; my eyesight and capacity to speak coherent sentences; my ability to spell; my chance to raise my daughter into resplendent womanhood and love my husband into replete self-acceptance; my heart-shaped desire to make an indelible difference; my unwritten books and unpublished poems; the seeds of promise I planted but never saw blossom; the years I use as yardsticks; my sequestered dreams and embryonic transformations; the view from old age. You halted me in my tracks when I had only made dents where I wanted to make craters and breezes where I wanted to blow storms. I thought you had come to kill me, not change me, to rob me, not enrich me, to clip my wings, not give me flight.

I was wrong. You have admonished me for treating my own well-being as an afterthought, not a priority, and bracketing my health with an arrogance equal only to my shame. You have shown me old insecurities I thought I had buried in the rebellions of my twenties and successes of my thirties, but now find lurking like sneak thieves in my cellar, ready to rob my hard-won self-regard in an instant. Like my fear of being too visible in case people notice my ordinariness or resent my extraordinariness. Like my belief that I am just too damn vulnerable and too damn weird and too damn honest to be let off my leash in public. No wonder I never engaged in social media until you came along, or published anything I'd ever written, or put my own name on what I do. I thought that would be narcissistic and self-indulgent. But now I see I was bending my life into an apology instead of arching it into an acclamation. Now I don't give a shit what other people resent me for. I give a shit about not crouching in the shadows or wasting precious particles of my God-given life.

My life wasn't actually tidy when you announced yourself. It was drifting. My best friend and business partner had recently walked away, in part because she recognized that I had lost my vision for what we had been doing together for twenty years. I had grown weary of teaching corporate executives and their employees how to shift their mind-sets when most of them just wanted a short-cut to success or a baton to beat their competitors with. A small minority who wanted to live fuller, nobler, more conscious lives, who recognized there was a more honoring, collaborative and humane way to do business, had made it worthwhile for many years, but much of the time it was like throwing pearls before swine. Arduous and largely thankless work, but well paid enough to keep at it long after my fire went out. My partner's exit forced me to notice the ashes of my original vision, but I was too hurt by the manner of her departure to sweep the ashes away or admit how burned-out I felt. It took you to help me do that. You forced me to stop work entirely and let the business I had built stand idle while I concentrated on saving my life. Then you inspired me anew, resurrecting the passions I had left on a shelf in my childhood and reshaping my vocation like a sculptor freeing a dancer from stone.

You crystallized my relationships very quickly. I had no time to pretend anymore, to please people I had little in common with or to hold on to stale friendships that had long since run their course. My boundaries became resolute and unapologetic, freeing me from social banter that merely pushed the air around, while restoring life-giving exchanges with the deep divers and the brave. At the same time, you brought home prodigal friends I had failed, forgotten and disappointed — the ones who knew me when I humiliated myself on the athletics track as a prematurely buxom teenager in the pre-sports-bra era and who forgave me my silence in the long years since.

Thanks to you, I have laid a place at my table for Grief, the friend I mistook for an intruder and left shivering in the cold when it sought shelter at my door. Now I have let it cascade through my memories and wash clean the hurts, losses and disappointments that you were able to latch on to when I was looking the other way.

Because of you, I have learned how toxic self-recrimination and regret are. You didn't just invite me to heal my body. You invited me to heal my entire relationship with myself. You have shown me what I can control and what I can't. You have resisted my demands for answers, predictability and the right to know what can, will and should happen to me. Instead, you walk me to the place where I fall off the cliff of my intelligence and drift on the gusts of The Great Unknown. You have made me set aside the husks of false beliefs, empty judgments and seductive lies. You have helped me trade comfort and certainty for awe and gratitude — not just for being alive (as if that weren't enough), but for the unsought, unwelcome things that shake the dead apples from my orchard, and the dark grief-soaked encounters where wonder is conjured and faith is born.

I am less lonely than I was before you begged me to pay attention to the deserted corners of my life. I am *here,* awake, alive, curious, leaning at an ever-steepening angle into the sheer beauty of living, taking nothing for granted and everything for grace.

Thank you, cancer.

For all of it.

Amen.

10
THE BEST MEDICINE

As well as I am doing with my cancer, and as experienced as I am at shifting my fear when it takes hold, I still have days when I am unable to do this. I don't want to do this "cancer thing" anymore. I don't want to google another treatment, take another supplement, attend another appointment or feel another cannula prick my tired veins. I don't want to be brave or noble or live in the moment, because tomorrow is no longer mine to take for granted. I want to eat chocolate, drink red wine, go back to work full-time and plan for the future as if I could count on it rising to meet me like the sun in the morning. I want to be normal. And well.

Recently, after an acutely painful episode of dealing with kidney stones, culminating in surgery and ten days of woe-is-me blues, I started eating chocolate and chips. I had been hypervigilant about my diet for ten months, but I hit the wall with this noncancer-related illness and fell off the wagon. I just didn't want to play anymore. I was done. I judged this behavior as self-indulgent and self-destructive, then spun off into a spiral of anxiety about feeding my tumors again and undoing the good work I had done. I don't know which was more toxic, the chocolate or the judgment. I do know that I couldn't pick myself up again without the support I have in my life.

On this occasion, support came again from my friend Catherine, who reminded me that I lost another seven pounds dealing with kidney stones and had dropped to an alarmingly low weight. She suggested that I was starving and that my body was begging me to introduce something new to my diet or at least to increase the amount I was eating. I needed to bulk up. Unconsciously, I reached out for sugar instead of listening to what my body really needed and adjusting my diet accordingly. I had needed someone to point that out to me, to reassure me that I hadn't done any irreversible damage and to help me get back on track.

This is how it goes. Navigating your own journey with cancer is an extraordinarily difficult thing to do. That's why so many patients place themselves in the hands of their oncologists without questioning the treatment being offered or exploring alternatives. Having cancer is a psychological minefield in which every decision can seem either life-threatening or lifesaving. Every mistake, or fear of one, can give you cause to pass the steering wheel back to the experts while you shuffle over into the passenger seat. If you choose to be "an exceptional patient" by becoming a specialist in your own care, then you need to put strong support systems in place — medical and emotional, personal and professional. This book is designed to help you stay at the wheel as much as possible, but please don't attempt to drive the whole distance alone.

In the supplement at the end of this book, you will find a list of resources and suggestions for your journey. But in addition to health practitioners and therapists, you need trusted friends and family members at your side. Ask some of them to read this book so they can be more informed as they help you navigate your journey by taking on some of the tasks, adopting the same mind-set, and reminding you of your purpose when you have ditched it in favor of the cookie jar. I haven't read all the books listed in the supplement from cover to cover. My husband, John, read some of them for me and distilled the most important or relevant information for me to use. He has taken up the slack wherever he can.

I met John when I was forty years old. It was at a leadership workshop in Oxfordshire when I was bent double with grief over the recent death of my beloved mentor, Brad, and was least expecting such resplendence. John was a quiet, potent presence among a group of twelve participants who assembled to explore the transformative nature of collaborative leadership. He dazzled me slowly, his beauty whispering in my ear while he sang bluegrass songs to the group, accompanied by his Martin guitar, and spoke with restrained dignity of his recently broken heart. He was grieving too. So we moved through the workshop discussions, collaborative exercises and vegetarian lunches as if the other didn't exist — consummate mourners keeping our respectful distances, but meeting in the margins where rapture might once more be possible and opposites make things whole.

John was yang to my yin and smooth to my rough, the square that mirrored my circle. No one noticed me snort in my stable when he explained how he had given up a well-remunerated job as a telecommunications company managing director to look after autistic children for eight pounds an hour. By the time he called me beautiful, while insisting he wasn't hitting on me, I very much wished he would. And, somehow, as the days unfolded, our individual griefs became a mutual longing that lifted us into a land where bitter and sweet were the same.

By our third date, maybe sooner, I knew I wanted to marry him. He cooked me dinner at his small one-bedroom apartment in Hertfordshire, which was simple and clean, with nothing extraneous. No TV, no paintings on the walls, no plump cushions on the sofa. Instead, there were two guitars, a well-worn mandolin, his beautifully lived-in face and the quiet power that inhabits those who belong to Something Else. After dinner, we went for an evening walk in a nearby park where the ground was thick with autumn leaves and the air was crisp with the anticipation of winter. We talked back and forth in a rhythm of mutual interest and exploration that flowed like a river around the bends in our lives while John picked up every piece of litter he saw on the ground before throwing it in each park trash can we walked by. He did so without fuss, fanfare or comment, as if he wasn't doing it at all. I was so focused on our conversation that we had left the park and were heading back to his apartment by the time I asked him why he was picking up trash on our early-days date when he was supposed to be concentrating entirely on me.

He explained that he kept finding money on the ground — ten pence here, a pound coin there — and it had started adding up, which was something he greatly appreciated now he was earning eight pounds an hour. So he decided to do a deal with Mother Earth by picking up a piece of trash for every penny he found. That same day he made this commitment, he found a five-pound note and a ten-pound note, his biggest haul to date, and so was still paying back the one thousand five hundred pieces of trash he consequently owed Mother Earth. Picking up trash became a feature of every date we went on, and would remain so, because that was the deal. And that was John. He collected and binned other people's litter willingly and joyously, as if he was collecting stranded starfish on an infinite beach and throwing them back in the sea. As if he was saving lives. By the time we exchanged vows and rings (which he couldn't afford to buy) seven months after our first meeting, I knew I was marrying a very wealthy man.

John's previous partner had been diagnosed with cancer just two months after the birth of their son, more than twenty years earlier. She lived through it and they later separated, so when I too was diagnosed with cancer, I was devastated to be putting John in the role of "carer" again after those hard years of caring for her. I wanted to free him from that role in life, from being the one in the background serving silently while the one in the foreground received all the love and attention. Now, here he was in that role again, this time with a young daughter and creakier bones. For a while it was almost more than I could bear to ask him to walk this path with me when I wanted him to be liberated, not laden, upheld, not upholding. Yet I was equally terrified of doing this without him — not the cancer so much as directing my own treatment and preserving my own personhood. I needed John at my side.

I remember him driving me to London for my second set of scan results. We already knew I had a tumor in my lung but didn't yet know if it had spread. My spirits were lighter than John's that day because I had let my terror break loose and shake its way through my body during a phone call with Catherine an hour before we left. I was prepared. He was still pent-up with it all, agitated and gloomy, trying to talk himself into optimism but not really pulling it off. He's like me — too in love with reality to get away with that shit and too ultimately faithful to the half-dark, half-light nature of Something Else.

As we drove toward Wandsworth from the A3, just where the two-lane highway narrows into a single lane and the traffic jams near the Royal Hospital for Neurodisability on West Hill, a hearse with large glass windows all around it pulled in front of us, carrying a gleaming wooden coffin covered in carefully woven wreaths of roses and lilies. The traffic was so slow that we were behind it for at least twenty minutes. At first, John pretended not to notice and tried to distract me with conversation, but the coffin appeared to me to be a bright banner with my name on it: God putting an elephant on our car hood, mentioning the unmentionable, spelling out on the blackboard what we both feared we were about to face.

"You've got to laugh," I said, hoping to lift his mood a bit before we arrived. "What would Life give us, eh? A coffin."

And laugh we did, all the way to the hospital where I received the PET scan results, which confirmed that my cancer had metastasized to my lymph nodes and bones.

We took the news calmly, together. Then we walked hand in hand to the place on the map where the map runs out, and began our remarkable voyage into the unknown.

Since then, John has been with me every inch of the way: chopping logs for the fire in front of which I sat for weeks in those early days, trying to wring the cold from my bones; driving to the biodynamic farm (an hour away) every week, to stock the fridge with food I can eat; taking our daughter on glorious adventures when I was too weak to hold her in my arms; watching the last remnant of light fade from my eyes when he told me Dr. Muñoz in Mexico (who I had heard doesn't turn patients down) wouldn't take me as a patient because of my brain tumors (but later did); curling up with me at night to savor the great love we had found, the scale of which could be matched only by the sorrow we felt at the prospect of leaving each other after too short an embrace on earth; preparing my three pots of supplements every day, and lining them up for me in the kitchen so I only take the one I need with each meal; fielding phone calls I didn't want to take and hosting visitors I didn't want to see; being here for me in a thousand ways I can neither quantify nor repay.

Above all else that I am grateful to him for, John has fully embraced the reality of what is happening to us without the denial and false positivity I find so wearing when I meet it. At the beginning some people kept telling me to "be positive" and "stay positive," but positivity can be as false as negativity and I didn't want to do that. I needed to be realistic about what was happening *now* without being presumptive about what was going to happen *next*. John understood this and stood for the reality of my diagnosis, even when others wanted to talk us out of it because they couldn't face it themselves. I remember him pacing up and down the lawn while on the phone to my mum, trying to get through to her about how serious my situation was. I had never heard him speak to her like that before. *No, it isn't like your friends who were cured of one tumor. No, it isn't reversible. No, she isn't going to do everything the doctors tell her. No, she isn't going to let them radiate her brain yet. No, it won't all be okay.* He just held the line with a firmness and faith in me for which I will love him forever.

"What Sophie decides to do is what we're going to do," he concluded emphatically during that call with my mum, who was understandably distressed about her daughter. "We need to trust her. She is the one who will find her way through this. She is in charge."

That's my babe. The one who gives me courage when I believe I can't keep going, who trusts my wisdom even when I am scrambling in the dark.

Not everyone has a John. I know that. I also know he couldn't have held so steady through all of this if we didn't have a wider network of support, including friends who reach past the glaring blaze of my more conspicuous needs for support to serve him in his own. We have created a cancer community around us, a group of friends, extended family, and professionals who are committed to serving us on this journey and without whom the crossing would be so much harder to undergo. This gift is greater than any I can requite. My hope is that our supporters feel enriched by the experience in some way, awakened by their encounters with our awakenings, and showered by their light that reflects off our awe.

Sometimes it can take cancer to bring down our walls and let people love us. It can take a life-threatening condition to make us confront our human condition — our ultimate fallibility and vulnerability, our deep-down longing for connection and community, the certainty of our kinship with the nature of things. This is the shell breaking and breathing in the ocean that it belongs to. And this is the whispering, the reaching into a well of darkness and finding your palms painted with light.

In the end, autonomy, courage and personhood are not enough. Not for me, at least. Not without partnership, friendship and intimacy. Not without love and support. Those things are not only *how* I get from A to B each day. They're *why*.

A few weeks ago, I was putting Gabriella to bed after her first tooth had fallen out, and she asked me, "What do we do when we die, Mummy?"

"Our souls leave our bodies and go to heaven," I replied without thinking. "Sometimes they come back to live in new bodies and sometimes they stay in invisible places on earth to love their children from."

"If you die, does that mean you're better?"

"No, darling, that would mean I didn't get better and you wouldn't be able to see or touch me anymore. But my soul would find an invisible place to love you from."

"Does dying hurt the soul, Mummy?"

"I don't think so, darling."

"Good. Because I love your soul,

Mummy," she said ever so softly before falling asleep with her tooth under the pillow, hoping the tooth fairy would come.

I live for those moments. Literally. I am pulled forward into life by love for my family and their love for me. This is the best medicine. When I am paralyzed by the "incurable" nature of my cancer and the belief that all I can do is buy a little more time, the seed of another possibility is pressed into my palm. The possibility of seeing my daughter blossom into adulthood and of offering my husband a shoulder to lean on when he is too bent and frail to cross the road alone.

At first I was completely unable to say the word "terminal" when describing my cancer, but later I stepped into it and zipped it up like a tight-fitting dress. I thought I needed to accept it and that using the term liberally would somehow strip the wind from its sails. And for a time it did. I even first entitled my blog *My Journey of Wellness with Terminal Illness,* which served its purpose for a while. But today, I choose to shed the label like a tree shedding its leaves for winter, ready to stand naked in the cold in the knowledge that spring will come. I don't need that word's protection anymore. I don't need the way I have let it define my journey and write my ending. I don't need to borrow its credentials to make my story one worth telling. We are all terminal, after all. I'm not so special. I am one of millions of cancer patients in the world right now, drinking from the well of our own wisdom as we stagger through the desert imbued with inescapable sorrow about our hemorrhaging safety. Our endings are not yet written and our wonderment is not yet stolen. So I place my pilgrimage with cancer on the altar of unknown hereafters, in the hope that it will rise like a moon over the darkened seas of our times.

EPILOGUE:
LIVING A THOUSAND LIVES

When *The Cancer Whisperer* was published in the UK, my life lit up like a solar flare. I hadn't anticipated the sweet spot it seemed to hit in the cancer culture or the way it would extend my reach with the work I had been teaching in other contexts for twenty years. People sought it out like wildebeest migrating toward seasonal rain. People who had no time to waste and no days to treat as dress rehearsals, whose resistances were already down and longings were already poignantly heightened. People whose life-threatening situations poised them for awakening and restoration and awe.

The steady flow of patients who contacted me seemed to have been waiting for a different dialogue about their illness: one that honored the truth of their experience and encouraged them to listen to, rather than battle, their disease. In addition to giving talks and running a few workshops, I started receiving e-mails and Facebook messages from complete strangers. Some shared their cancer stories with me as if I were a family member or a priest. Some reached out to me from the pit of their despair because they didn't know where else to take it. Others simply wrote to say thank you, "for saying it the way I want it said."

I neither planned it nor foresaw it. I didn't push for it, either. I resisted pressure to "build a platform" to reach more people, because that wasn't my agenda. I was following what was unfolding more than driving it, and this strategy was important. It made the process manageable and kept me grounded. I could serve selectively, while protecting my own well-being. After all, I was still gravely ill and needed to keep following my protocols, though these inevitably lapsed at times. But mostly I felt well. I was showing up, shining my light, and making a difference. I wasn't just alive. I was living the life I had almost walked out on before my taken-for-granted tomorrows suddenly walked out on me. I called this period "The Reprieve."

It might have been easy to slip into denial with all this excitement going on, but it isn't like that. Not when your cancer is stage four. It's always part of the landscape, like a black lake in a prairie basin. Sometimes it spreads out for miles in front of you as you arrive, legs burning, at the top of a steep ridge on a mountain climb. Other times, when the terrain levels out for a while, it dips behind a ridge you haven't reached yet, almost entirely hidden from view. In these times, I feel so normal I can catch my breath and cool my muscles, as I used to on childhood walks in the Black Mountains of South Wales, where the soft grass, thick heather, and acres of dense forestry rolled out like a green storm as far as the eye could see. I take in fine details of a view I would likely have overlooked in my carefree, precancerous days: the way the clouds roll like a tide along the bottom of the valley, crashing on the low shores of distant foothills, or the creamy crescent moon rises in daylight and hangs in the blue sky like an angel's trumpet; the way tame horses graze on cropped pastures of cultivated farmlands, and wild horses roam in herds across the vaulted ridges, their long manes flying behind them in the cool breeze that blows through the mountain corridors; the way sunlight turns gold when it burns through black clouds during the hangover after a storm.

Then, as night falls and the distractions of

daytime are slowly silenced, the lake appears again just behind your left shoulder and, in the corner of your eye, you catch the moonlight painting silver streaks across its shimmering surface.

Cancer is a presence. A constant, relentless, unforgiving presence. It won't be denied or forgotten for very long — even between the rolling ridges, where the ground flattens and your muscles stop burning and it isn't going to kill you today.

Nor can I forget it because I belong to a tribe now. The cancer tribe. We are everywhere. We are sitting on trains, driving on freeways, walking our dogs in the park. We meet one another in hospital waiting rooms and chemo wards. We find one another in online support groups. We connect in natural health centers and alternative clinics, many of which continue taking risks to treat us because the Cancer Police (aka Trading Standards, a UK legal enforcement body) are always on the hunt to shut them down.

You can identify some of us by our wigs and turbans, or the gray pallor of our skin when we start dying, but many of us still have full heads of hair and look as healthy as any other passerby. We wear our illnesses like undergarments, mostly hoping no one will notice but sometimes wishing they would.

We can spot one another more easily, of course. We know the signs: the thinning eyebrows; the short crop of new hair; the well-worn veins; the portacath just below the neckline of someone's shirt, or the small scar where one used to be. "Where's your primary?" we ask, often before introducing ourselves. "What stage?" Sometimes we simply announce our particular diseases, as if they are our names: "Liver. Stage three." "Prostate. With bone mets." "Lung. Stage four." "Breast. BRCA gene." "Mesothelioma. Contained." It's all we need to say to begin a dialogue about the dreams and dreads that now furnish our cherished days.

There's no ducking cancer once you've joined the tribe, although it's easier to distance yourself from it in the earlier stages. A late-stage diagnosis seems to tip some patients into a deeper acceptance of their condition and an unmentionable envy of those who caught it earlier. We are a tribe within the tribe. We are the ones who cower a little when we hear inspiring stories of remission and recovery, truly heartened by those who have turned it around but fearful that we live on the sidelines of that playing field, believing we're unable to claim victory in a narrative where the only "winners" are survivors. Largely the press drives this narrative, but it also derives from the relative lack of funding for metastasized cancer and a medical system that has long written off late-stage patients. This is slowly beginning to change, but it can be very dispiriting to be set up as inevitable "losers" even as we cut our deepest veins of courage, humor, and awe. In less than two years, I have known and lost several of these cancer warriors, squeezing profound friendships out of the few months, weeks, or even hours between our meeting and their passing. Each death brands me like a hot iron, leaving me permanently tattooed by their tenacity and dignity and grace.

Sometimes I feel so angry, so confounded by the way this one makes it and that one doesn't. I feel especially angry when we lose the moms of wee ones like my girl. Occasionally, I wonder why I'm still alive when they're not. I slip into survivor's guilt as into a silk nightgown and lie down in it until morning. Then I rise to embrace another day. I turn my attention to the living and thriving, to the unexpected recoveries against the odds and the low murmur of the miraculous whistling through the wind.

Not that I'm officially a survivor. That

term is reserved for those who have been in remission at least five years, and remission is a ridge I may never reach on this particular trail, however strenuously I strive for it. Nearly two years after my diagnosis, I am still aiming for the mountain peak I paint in my dreams: the place where I wake up without cancer casting its shadow across my morning and its mist across my gaze. The place where I am scooped up by a heroic universe and find myself inexplicably cured.

Instead, my brain tumors came back. A lot of brain tumors.

I found out in April 2016. Gabriella had just turned six and was in a state of wide-eyed wonder because Joy, her favorite character in the Disney Pixar film *Inside Out* (and her alter ego), had come to her party *in person* to entertain her friends. Imagine that! My book had just been auctioned to U.S. publishers, a second book had been commissioned, and I was preparing to celebrate my fiftieth birthday in style. I had, at long last, fallen completely in love with my life.

In my forty-nine years on earth, I had fallen in love with bougainvillea, Mahatma Gandhi, the Greek island of Lesvos, the Okavango Delta, peonies, champagne on starlit beaches, horse rides in the Andes and the Arizona desert, the Red Rock mountains of Sedona, the bead-throwing Mardi Gras revelers of New Orleans, Maya Angelou, Atticus, Heathcliff, the Garden of England (a county called Kent, southeast of London, where I now live), my husband, my daughter, truth-tellers, justice crusaders, deep feelers, conscience carriers, the version of God I encounter in lifeshocks rather than religious texts and places of worship, and our wondrous little planet spinning in infinite space. I had fallen in love with a hundred poems, a hundred places, and a hundred lives, but I hadn't fallen in love with my own. It took cancer to help me do that.

Of course, we don't fall in love. We rise. This is the measure of how real love is. We are more, not less, of ourselves in its presence. We are uplifted, not laid low. For all the devastation of those early weeks after my diagnosis, cancer became the unexpected hand that banished my self-forgetfulness and pulled me into legitimate self-regard. It burned the bushels I had been hiding my light under. It ripped off the "too-muchness" I had worn like an invisible cloak because "not-enoughness" seemed so much more acceptable. It pulled me up on my sellouts and fall-shorts. It made me rise in love with myself.

So why was my disease progressing now? From a medical perspective it's quite common. The blood-brain barrier is notoriously hard to penetrate, so the brain is often the first to resist medication that continues to control the cancer elsewhere. But from a "whispering" perspective, why now? Had all this unexpected attention, from the media as well as fellow patients, come a little too close for comfort without my realizing? Did I want to crawl back under my bushel, where I was safe in my anonymity and no one was looking to me for inspiration, guidance, or hope? Was I still mildly allergic to being shiny and visible? Was the sun that blazed down on me beginning to burn?

I needed to work out a treatment plan, yes, but my brain tumors begged these questions too. They turned my attention inward again until I realized part of me had grown uneasy. I thought I had dropped my shame like a hot stone into a deep well, where it lay lost and irretrievable. Not so. Quite unconsciously, I had started looking for shelter from the tumult, in the cool shade cast by low-hanging branches of weeping trees, which veiled my simmering self-reproach. A small, scared, deeply embarrassed part of me wanted out. Not out of life but out of the limelight and all the emotional burdens I feared it would make me bear.

The news came, as all news does, in a series of lifeshocks following a routine MRI scan. First, a call from Tim, my regular oncologist, to say, "We have a real problem, Mrs. Sabbage." Then, there were the four visible tumors I could see on the scan in his office and "several tiny spots indicating there could be more." Then hearing the "standard treatment" — a term he emphasized more than once as if it would persuade me to accept rather than reject it — that "usually controls the cancer for ten months."

"No," I finally responded after leaning in and taking in and hanging in. "We need to find another way."

And so began the next deep-dive inquiry into what might be possible if I was aiming higher than the standard ten months. I interrogated him for more than an hour that day — about cognitive capacities and motor functions I was in danger of losing, trials I might participate in, drugs that penetrate the blood-brain barrier, tests he hadn't even heard of, and experimental strategies we might try.

By now I had a bit more legal leverage.

The Access to Medical Treatments Act —
the offspring of Lord Saatchi's Medical Innovation Bill, which had been thrown out
by the coalition government Health Minister
in 2014 — had since been passed in the UK
Parliament by the newly elected Conserva-
tive majority government. This shaft of light
allows seriously ill patients to access a medical database containing details of all new
medicines in development and volunteer for
innovative treatment. I had no idea if this
would be relevant to me but was quick to
remind him of this new law when he cau-
tioned me about experimenting.

To his credit, my dear, flexible, forbearing
oncologist met me with no pushbacks or
put-downs, which is how it has been this
time around. I've had numerous medical
meetings with several conventional doctors
about my brain since that day, and something has changed. I'm not hitting walls,
meeting resistance, or being patronized by
experts who want me to do what I am told.
Instead, I am being related to as a person,
not a patient; a human being, not an illness;
the director, not the recipient, of my treatment.

In the end, I decided I needed a brain
expert more than a cancer expert and found
a witty neurosurgeon in London who of-

fered me Gamma knife radiation. This involves having a metal frame screwed to your skull prior to treatment — which is intensely uncomfortable but not as bee-stingingly painful as the anesthetic injections that precede it. Unlike whole-brain radiotherapy, which radiates the brain indiscriminately, this frame is fitted to bolt your head into the machine and keep it completely still while they target the lesions with minute accuracy and thus protect the surrounding tissue. In my case, this lasted eight hours.

On the day of treatment, my brain was scanned again with a very-fine-cut MRI machine that detects lesions standard machines don't. We anticipated somewhere between eight and twelve small tumors. They found twenty-seven.

Later, my neurosurgeon told me it was unlikely this treatment would have been approved if so many tumors had been detected when I first went to see him. His eyes twinkled with delight because we had bucked the system and biffed the whole lot in one session. Apparently, I now hold the record for the number of lesions targeted in a single treatment at that hospital. And there, yet again, by the grace of Something go I.

A lot of people have asked how I handled lying still for eight hours straight. I took a couple of breaks and threw up in one of them. I also lay there observing my mind-talk and working through multiple layers of fear for quite some time. After that it became surprisingly peaceful. This may have been helped by new infusions I have been receiving from a natural health practitioner who diagnosed a chronic weakness in my nervous and endocrine systems after a long period of sustained trauma. This wasn't a word I would have used until she did. Like most cancer patients, I had become used to all the drugs, scans, blood tests, supplements, side effects, procedures, protocols, contrast dyes, cannulas, and countless bloody needles in our weary, thinning veins. I have infusions in my ankles these days. But her approach has reminded me that it matters to acknowledge the built-up effect of all these small but relentless blows, and that my body still needs permission to release the unacknowledged traumas that mark some of the ridges I have climbed in the past fifty years. It has been a deep, sanity-preserving, adrenal-soothing relief.

But more than this, I trusted the lifeshocks that day. I opened up to them like ghost flowers open to bees in the Mojave Desert.

I trusted the team of doctors and nurses who monitored my brain on the computer so attentively that they forgot to offer me a glass of water. Equally, I forgot to ask. I felt anxious for a while, but much of the time I thought about Gabriella and the accumulated wisdoms I still wanted to pass on to her. I meditated, contemplated, and prayed until my emotional stillness matched my physical stillness. And I started to envision my next book. Before I knew it, the procedure was over and I was internally renewed.

The aftermath was brutal. It was like coming home from a day on a scorching hot beach with no sunscreen, only to realize that your skin is severely burned. Except the sunburn is inside your head. And the pain lasts for weeks. I tried to ride it out with ibuprofen but eventually resorted to the dreaded steroids, which really helped. My fears about taking them were fully realized, though: sleepless nights, rapid weight gain, and sugar cravings that were hard to control. I stopped as soon as I could.

Just three weeks later, I celebrated my fiftieth birthday. I threw a huge party in a marquee in our garden, attended by a hundred and fifty people from every decade of my life. I suspect some came because it might be their last chance to see me, but there was nothing somber about the evening. It was an epic expression of gratitude for all the ways they had imprinted my heart and marked my soul since I arrived in the world. It was an unbridled celebration of life. Just after dinner, we brought out a hundred and fifty African drums, passed them to every guest at every table and, orchestrated by my friend Tom Morley — who was once the drummer in a popular UK '80s band called Scritti Politti — drummed in perfect unison, as if we were drumming for every human being with cancer who is walking, and has walked, upon this earth. I wore a long ivory fit-and-flare dress that night, hand-crocheted by Peruvian artisans in an elaborate web of daisies, as if I was marrying myself. I hitched it up to put the drum between my knees and, as I felt the rhythm crescendo all around me, an almighty pressure popped in my chest until I roared like a mountain waterfall. Not with rage, grief, or even relief, but joy. Simple, unexpected, unadulterated joy. It was one of the high points of my life.

During the evening, my guests wrote messages in "Say It to Sophie" books created for the occasion, which I feasted on in the days after. It was like reading what people might say at my funeral, but I was privileged to hear it all before the sand in my timer ran out. One of the messages that most touched me was from my brother, which simply read:

Sis. You have no idea how proud you have made me, I don't cease to be stunned by what you have achieved in these last eighteen months and the incredible way you are living life with such intensity that it is like you are living a thousand lives. I love you.

Your Big Bro.

Living a thousand lives. I love that. Before cancer, time was thin. I lost it regularly. Whole days would pass by without my making something of them. Other days were packed with busyness, but no presence, no savoring the bounty of a moment. *This breath. This breeze. This word as it falls on this page.* I had even taught a few time management courses in large corporations as if that were even possible, as if you could save time or steal time or bottle it in a jar.

In a crisis, time gets fat. It fills up seconds with eternities until they spill over like brimful vases. It draws out like an ocean or opens, layer by layer, like a peony. It's similar to that moment when you finally kiss someone you've been aching for and then melt into so much tenderness that time stands still and bows.

A cancer diagnosis doesn't make you more important than the rest of our mortal race. Any one of us can be taken out at any moment — gunned down in a nightclub while we're dancing, mown down by a truck when we're celebrating an annual summer festival with our children, washed away by an ocean we're trying to cross in a desperate bid for freedom. But it does put you on notice. It focuses your experience. It compels you to walk tenaciously and faithfully toward an unknown summit you may never reach. It invites you to live a thousand lives in whatever time you are granted, without ever really knowing how much time that is.

This discovery of twenty-seven tumors in my brain, and the consequent treatment, has been an acutely sobering encounter with my fragility. Less than three months later they have almost completely disintegrated, but for a few barely visible spots that my neurosurgeon assures me are on the way out as well. It will just take a little more time for them to disappear. Better yet, no new lesions have appeared, which means the disease is in check again, and my options for future treatment are not exhausted.

Naturally, I am awash with gratitude and relief.

When I'd heard the number twenty-seven, I felt deeply shaken, as if by an earthquake tremor, and yet strangely soothed at the same time. Later, I discovered that the number twenty-seven represents the trinity of trinities: three times three times three. The number of the Holy Spirit. Perhaps I am grasping at straws, but this brought me great solace, a deep sense of being held by Something Greater and of a secret sacred code embedded in the stars.

Twenty-seven is also a lunar number, indicating light in the darkness. I remember my beloved mentor, Brad Brown, telling me that it is less significant to bring light *to* the darkness — as so many gurus in this over-crowded spiritual marketplace purport to do — than to find light *in* the darkness, which is where the divine light resides. I have come to trust, with every fiber of my being, that the light is there even when I cannot see it, that it is permanent and count-on-able, and that even as I fumble through the shadows to find it, it is reaching through the dense fog of my blinding fearfulness and will not rest until it finds me.

APPENDIX: SUPPORT SYSTEMS

I am a cancer patient, not a doctor or health practitioner. As such, I cannot prescribe or recommend specific health interventions for you or your journey with cancer. You need to take complete responsibility for your research into different treatments and which ones you choose to use. I also recommend that you seek expert medical advice when putting your treatment plan together.

However, since my own research took many weeks, I would have greatly appreciated some guidance about resources so that I didn't need to spend many hours separating the wheat from the chaff. In order to give you some shortcuts through the mass of information out there, I'll share here the resources that have made the most difference to me.

This includes a list of alternative treatments I use to complement my radiotherapy and the tumor-inhibiting drug prescribed by my oncologist, which I take every day. If any of the treatments seems like a good fit for you, I hope you can find practitioners you like and ways to source their services.

DOCUMENTARIES

1. *Cancer Conquest,* a documentary by Burton Goldberg: www.burtongoldberg.com/catalog/cancer-21
2. *Surviving Terminal Cancer,* a Patient Advocacy Film that charts the story of Ben Williams, who was diagnosed with the most lethal form of cancer known to medicine and is still alive twenty years later. A Waking Giant Production. www.survivingterminalcancer.com

BOOKS

1. *The Cancer Revolution: Integrative Medicine, The Future of Cancer Care,* Patricia Peat with 37 expert contributors (Win-Win Health Intelligence Ltd, 2016)
2. *50 Critical Cancer Answers,* Francisco Contreras, MD, and Daniel E. Kennedy, MC (Authentic Publishers, 2013)
3. *Radical Remission,* Kelly A. Turner (HarperCollins, 2014)
4. *You Are the Placebo,* Dr. Joe Dispenza (Hay House, 2014)
5. *Beating Cancer: Twenty Natural, Spiritual,*

and *Medical Remedies,* Francisco Contreras, MD, and Daniel Kennedy, MD (Si-
loam, 2010)
6. *Anti Cancer: A New Way of Life,* David
   Servan-Schreiber, MD, PhD (Penguin
   Books, 2007)
7. *Anatomy of an Illness,* Norman Cousins
   (W. W. Norton and Company, 1979)
8. *Head First: The Biology of Hope,* Norman
   Cousins (Penguin Books USA, 1989)
9. *Cancer: Increasing Your Odds for Survival,*
   David Bognar (Hunter House, 1998)
10. *You Can Fight for Your Life: Emotional
    Factors in the Treatment of Cancer,* Law-
    rence LeShan (Thorsons Publishers Ltd,
    1984)

Note: These books are listed pretty much in
the order I recommend reading them. I do
not agree with everything in these books,
but I did find wisdom in all of them that
has been of use to me. Always remember to
use your own wisdom when assessing the
advice of others!

TREATMENTS

This is a list of all the treatments I have
used in my self-designed program, most of
which can be easily researched and sourced
online. Some — like cannabis oil — are

harder to find access to (you can now find cannabis oil, also known as hemp oil, more easily than in the past, and most cancer communities can tap you into a source).

Rife technology can also be tricky to find, especially if you want to be confident in what you are paying for, because the machines are expensive. Rife technology uses machines that put out sound frequencies to attack microbes in the cancer cells as well as in the blood (www.introductiontorife .com).

From clinics in Mexico:
1. Hyperthermia
2. Ozone therapy
3. Mega doses of vitamin C
4. Mega doses of laetrile (also known as amygdalen and vitamin B17)
5. The Dendritic Vaccine

From alternative health practitioners:
1. Acupuncture
2. Chinese herbs
3. Colonic irrigation
4. Naturopathy
5. Anticancer nutrition
6. Lymph drainage massage
7. Hot stone massage
8. Far infrared saunas
9. Kinesiology

At-home treatments and support:
1. Rife technology (see note on the previous page for more information)
2. Cannabis oil
3. Coffee enemas (for detoxing and to stimulate liver and gall bladder function)
4. Castor oil packs (for detoxing)
5. Foot soaks and mud packs (for detoxing)
6. Epsom salt and bicarbonate of soda baths (for detoxing)
7. Oxygen machine (for use with exercising) or hyperbaric oxygen therapy
8. EMR (electromagnetic radiation) blockers on electronic devices
9. Green juices made with a juicing machine
10. Meditation
11. Hypnotherapy

Psychological and spiritual treatments:
1. Psychotherapy
2. Brain mapping and neurofeedback
3. Shamanic healing
4. Constellation work
5. Personal coaching
6. Grief counseling

CLINICS AND PRACTITIONERS

This list does not include all my personal practitioners. There are plenty of practitioners around for those treatments, so you will need to source them in your own area. These are the practitioners whose permission I have to include them in this book. You can go to their websites to find out more about what they offer:

1. Dr. Dana Flavin: www.collmed.org
2. The Oasis of Hope Hospital, Mexico, Dr. Francisco Contreras: www.oasisofhope.com
3. The San Diego Clinic, Mexico, Dr. Filberto Muñoz: www.sdiegoclinic.com
4. The first title in my book list, *The Cancer Revolution,* is the other book (apart from this one) that I couldn't find when diagnosed. It includes a comprehensive list of integrative treatments as well as lists of the best clinics around the world. It also includes a list of books to read if you need more guidance. I trust the authors and the research they have done. You can buy it at thecancerrevolution.co.uk.

SUPPLEMENTS

There is an enormous range of supplements you could take to support your health, but it is essential you identify these with a qualified practitioner. It is also important to be tested and assessed by a professional, but you can look into all this with nutritionists, naturopaths, and doctors at integrated clinics. It took me several weeks to determine my own program of supplements and I review it every few months, so be patient with the process of finding supplements that work for you. It can take some time to figure out.

CONTINUING YOUR JOURNEY WITH ME

I hope this book has made a difference to you in its own right. It was written to do so. However, if you would like to continue your journey with me and connect to a cancer-whispering community, you are welcome to:

1. Follow my blog: sophiesabbage.com/blog.
2. Learn about other events on offer at sophiesabbage.com/events.
3. Sign up for notifications of blog posts, free downloads (including my "Trace the Roots of Your Cancer" videos and questionnaire), and news of future events at www.sophiesabbage.com.
4. Follow my Cancer Whisperer Facebook page at www.facebook.com/thecancer whisperer.
5. Ask to join my Facebook support group, the Cancer Whisperers, at www.facebook .com/groups/282379948763905.

ACKNOWLEDGMENTS

I have dedicated this book to my husband, John Sabbage, and my mentor, Dr. K. Bradford Brown, because I believe I would not still be here without the love of the former and the teachings of the latter. However, I could not have written this book or, indeed, lived long enough to write this book without the support — loving, bold, tender and practical — of some other remarkable people. I especially want to thank:

My parents, Nick and Ann Crickhowell, for trusting me to direct my own treatment on this journey, even when it terrified them — and for the numerous ways they have supported me since I was diagnosed.

My siblings, Rupert Edwards and Olivia Clarke, for showing up so lovingly when I needed them most and being willing to pick up the most precious pieces of my life if I don't make it.

Catherine Rolt, for being my best friend through this whole journey and my inspiration about how to thrive with a debilitating disease. Her spirit burns brighter than almost any I know and her courage is a wonder to behold.

Kitty de la Beche, for seeing my future when I couldn't and helping me build a platform to be of service again.

Rosie Jackson, for her deliciously truthful feedback about the first draft of this book. More importantly, for being my spiritual sister since tutoring me at university and transforming my relationship with God.

Dr. Tim Sevitt, Dr. Francisco Contreras, Dr. Dana Flavin, Dr. Michael Sandberg, Dr. Peter Harper and Dr. Filberto Muñoz. Lifesavers all.

Stuart Camp, Sanna Carapellotti, Fiona Corliss, Amanda Day, Cherry Jarrett, Mr. Lee, John Tindall and Grover Wonderlin for serving my body, mind and heart on this journey. Spirit savers all.

Elaine Alpert for sharing her remarkable healing skills with me so generously, which nourished my spirit as much as my body, in addition to her steadfast and treasured friendship.

Peggy Jarrett and David Temper for their unwavering love, listening and generosity in my darkest hours.

Andrea Constantine for moving in when I was dying and not leaving until I came back to life.

My amazing and beautiful agent, Valeria Huerta, who showed up on my doorstep having read my book and promised to share it with the world. A true spiritual warrior.

Mark Booth, my publisher at the Coronet imprint of Hodder & Stoughton, for seeing something in my book he wanted to bring forth to the world and for seeing me as a writer first, teacher second, and cancer patient third. I am privileged to be one of his authors.

Becky Cole, my editor at Plume, for bringing this book to North America and seeing the poet in me as well as the cancer warrior. She understood the nature of "life-shocks" from the start of our relationship and continues to engage with them in our professional interactions and creative process.

All the team at Penguin Random House for putting their energy, passion, and expertise behind this book and for recognizing the difference it could make on their side of the big pond.

Angela Lauria, who started me off on this publishing journey, for her fierce vision and deep care and for providing a platform for me to launch my career as a writer who can make a difference.

Grace Kerina, for editing the first edition of my e-book. She is her name — grace personified.

Veronica Nathan, for showing up like an angel when my family was in dire straits to clear my clutter, clean our home, and relieve the domestic pressure in a hundred ways.

Sharon Agates, Andrew Baker, Susan Ball, Greg Barton, Kate Bartholomew, Andrea Bolton, Charlie Bower, Anne Brown, Linda Brown, Sahera Chohan, Tom Colquitt, Hermione Crosfield, Lydia Dickinson, Simon Fernyhough, Anja Fiedler, Liz Digby-Firth, Frances and Adrian Grant, Mikey Lewis, Clare Lucas, Karen Luckhurst, Peter Lurie, Diane Makens, Alison Maley, Nick May, Annabel Moeller, Gerry Moline, Amanda Nicol, Susanne Olbrich, Miho Pickering, Alison Pope, Sarah Stephens, Dave Tomlinson, Bill Torbert, Lorena Sanz, Jane Slemeck, Jane Wedlake and Brocas Walton for their many acts of friendship and kindness, big and small. They are my village.

The mums, dads, and teachers at my daughter Gabriella's school for the playdates, school lifts, and moral support through such a difficult time.

And all those who have contributed financially to my medical treatments, most of whom prefer not to be named. I am immeasurably grateful.

ABOUT THE AUTHOR

Sophie Sabbage is a writer, speaker, and facilitator who has worked in the field of human development, mind-set transformation, and corporate culture change since 1994. Since being diagnosed with late-stage lung cancer in October 2014, Sophie has drawn on her wisdom, courage, and tenacity to create her life anew.

In addition to running her own businesses — Interaction (www.interactionuk.com) and Sophie Sabbage Ltd (sophiesabbage .com) — Sophie has been a senior trainer with the educational charity More To Life (moretolife.org.uk) since 2001.

An insatiable student who was crawling up bookshelves at the age of two, Sophie achieved a first-class BA in English literature and psychology before going on to study various approaches to human and organizational change over a number of years. She measures leadership not by how many followers one has but by how many other leaders one creates. Her British passport and right to vote are among her most prized possessions.

Sophie is very happily married to John Sabbage and is the proud mother of their daughter, Gabriella.